The Tomm
from South
Brent

The Tommies from South Brent

Bernard Elms

First Published in 2016 by R&J Press

Thank you to the family of James Clark for agreeing to use his painting in this publication, *The Great Reward.*

British Library Cataloguing in Publication Data:A catalogue record for this book is available from the British Library

ISBN: 978-0-9955309-0-4

Publication managed by TJ INK www.tjink.co.uk

Printed and bound in Great Britain by TJ International, Padstow, Cornwall

Cover Illustration

My thanks go to Ann Chambers, whose painting 'Poppies and WW1 Soldiers' illustrates the cover of this book. It depicts soldiers advancing through the poppy fields of the Western Front.

Ann trained in graphic art and worked in the printing trade. After her marriage she lived in Grantham but now resides in Nottinghamshire. She has displayed locally for several years and has exhibited in London. Ann Says:

> *"I love painting! There is no greater pleasure for me than to have a blank canvas, loads of paint and the radio playing my favourite music. When I start to paint I deliberately have no idea what I am going to produce."*

For more information go to www.annchambers.net

Table of Contents

Introduction

South Brent has been referred to as a large village or a small town situated in the Avon Valley between the city of Plymouth, to the west and Exeter to the east, nestling on the edge of the Dartmoor National Park in South Devon. It is predominantly a rural community but at the time of the Great War there was a lot of local industry with Flock and Corn mills operating along the banks of the river Avon, regular markets and sheep sales were held in the town.

4th August 2014 marks the centenary of the commencement of hostilities in Europe between the German Empire under Kaiser Wilhelm and The British Empire. This event became one of the longest, bloodiest, continual wars in history, with great loss of life on both sides.

Great Britain with all the members of the Commonwealth will commemorate this event in their own particular way, here in the village of South Brent as in many towns and villages throughout the country there will be some form of commemoration. This work forms part of our village commemoration.

For our part here in the village of South Brent, Devon, we will be thinking of the men and woman who went to war, some never to return and will evermore be resting in a foreign land, as well as those who are buried here in village.

This work will look at all the men and woman commemorated on the War memorial plaque in St Petroc's Church placed there in July 1920, as an act of remembrance by the parish and bereaved families of South Brent as well as men and women from Rattery, Avonwick, Diptford and the surrounding hamlets. Not all those named on the memorial were born in the village, many were resident here at the outbreak of hostilities.

We will be looking at the reports in the local newspapers, National Archives, school memorials and other Church and village memorials where the names of South Brent men appear.

The format of the book will look briefly at the political turmoil that started the war, the pressures that men and the local communities were subjected 'to encourage' men to enlist into the services, the men and women who died in the conflict and, as far as possible, a list of men who served and returned to their homes. All footnoted items are shown at the end of the relevent section or chapter.

All the men and women who died in the '*War to end all Wars*' are mentioned in biographical detail as far as possible. The men who went to war and returned home to the parish are listed in chapter seven from press cuttings and other forms of records available.

There is a possibility that not all the details will be correct as a lot of the records are not as accurate as they could be, or they were destroyed or damaged in later conflicts. In this case if there are any members of the families mentioned who have either additional material or are able to correct any error I would be very pleased to put the record straight.

Some of the extracts from the local papers and records have different spellings not commonly used with differing grammatical meanings to what we are used to today. I have quoted the spellings and grammar used at the time to illustrate the tone of language used in the early 1900's.

The names of the men and women who died during the Great War are listed in this work as their names appear in the Church Memorial and not in a strict alphabetical order.

St Petroc's Church, South Brent. (Photo Author)

Acknowledgements

During the research of this book I have been in contact with many people and organisations.

My personal thanks to the following:

Firstly to my wife Jill, for her support and encouragement;
Mrs Jean Sandry, Mrs Margaret Eales, Mrs Rene Cranch;
Mrs Lynette Gribble, Miss Dorothy-Rose Gribble,
Ms Diana Goodman;
Mrs Angela Young, Rowland Archives;
Mr Greg Wall;
Mr Conrad Heath;
Mr W. Douglas, The Douglas Archive;
South Brent Council Archives;
The Totnes Times, formerly The Totnes and Mid Devon News;
The National Achieves, Kew, London;
Devon County Archive, Exeter;
Harrow School Archive;

Without their help and assistance the names of the men and women commemorated in the Parish Church would remain just names and those men whose names were never recorded in the Church would remain lost forever.

Preface

'The public has a right to expect from us that we should place a firm confidence in the gallantry and discipline of the troops under our command, and I have the satisfaction of reflecting that, having tried them frequently, they never failed me'.

(Duke of Wellington at the height of
the Peninsular War in Spain 1807-1814.)

It is clear that Wellington's words ring true of the men and women who enlisted for service in 1914-1918, and it is the responsibility of the later generations to remember the sacrifices made by them, to encourage future generations that the best way to settle disputes is not war but dialogue.

The Remembrance Services for the fallen of the Great War take place throughout the country, and within the dominions of the old British Empire, in November every year. The names of the fallen are read out and two minutes silence is observed to remember the events of that era. There are now no survivors from the war alive, and I am aware of only one lady who is the daughter of one soldiers killed that is still with us. Now one hundred years later the names on the South Brent Church Memorial sadly, are only names, *The Last 'Tommy'* Mr Harry Patch, has now passed away. These men and women are only remembered in the annals of family history with perhaps their war medals and a photograph their only reminders.

During the 1970's there were moves to phase out the annual Remembrance Day and associated pageantry that went with it. It was felt that the Great War was long over and society should move on. The Falklands war of 1982 and more recent conflicts which British servicemen and women have been involved and died, has renewed a patriotic interest of the British military and its conflict's where servicemen and women have died.

The advent of the computer and the internet and the digitising of all types of records has made genealogy and family history a very popular hobby, this and the fact the school curriculum now includes the study of war and conflict has further strengthened the argument for the retention of the Remembrance Day ceremonies.

This work is aimed at recounting the events of the men and women from South Brent who joined the colour's and served their country in a time of need and died for that cause.

Raj Mohan Gandhi, grandson of Mahatma Gandhi said: '*History is often made by people usually missed out by historians*'.

Terms and Abbreviations Used

A.I.F.	Australian Imperial Force
A.S.C	Army Service Corps
B.E.F.	British Expeditionary Force
C.E.F.	Canadian Expeditionary Force
Capt.	Captain
CDr	Commander (RN)
Cpl.	Corporal
D.C.L.I.	Duke of Cornwall's Light Infantry
G.C.	General Command
G.H.Q,	General Head Quarters
Gnr.	Gunner
GWR.	Great Western Railway
H.M.S.	His Majesty Ships
Lt.	Lieutenant
M.G.C.	Machine Gun Corps.
MID.	Mentioned in Dispatches
MM.	Military Medal
P.O.W.	Prince of Wales
P.M.C.	Plymouth and Mannameadian College
Pte. *or* Pvt.	Private (Soldier)
Q.M.A.A.C	Queen Mary's Army Auxiliary Corps.
R.E.	Royal Engineers
R.F.A.	Royal Field Artillery.

R.F.C.	Royal Flying Corps.
R.G.A.	Royal Garrison Artillery
R.M	Royal Marine
R.N.	Royal Navy
Sgt.	Sergeant.
V.A.D.	Voluntary Aid Detachment
V.T.C.	Volunteer Training Corps
W.G.C.	War Graves Commission

Chapter One

The Men and Women of South Brent who died in the Great War

1. The following list is the list of names of those who died in the Great War and are commemorated in St Petrock's[1] Church, South Brent.

Cpl. Henry Abbott.
Anti. Air Craft Section.
Cpl. Henry Knott. R. G. A
2nd Lt G. Butcher. North Staffs.
Cpt. Colin Langford. RFC
Lt. Jasper Carew. West York's
Stoker Walter Mortimore RN
Pte. Ernest Farleigh. Grenadier. Guards
Pte. Raymond Newman. DCLI
Cdr. Cecil France-Hayhurst. RN
Pte. Joseph Oliver. ASC.
Major Hugh F, Glanville. 1ST West Indian Regt. RFC.
Pte. Edwin P. M. Goss. Devon's
Pte. John E. Salter. Devon's.
Lt. Charles H, Gribble. The Buffs
(Royal East Kent Regt.)
L/Cpl. Leonard H. Shillabeer. Devon's

Trooper. Henry Bennett Gribble.
Canadian Mounted Rifles.
L/Cpl. Bertie Hard. M. G. C.
Pte. George Smallridge, Devon's
Pte. Benjamin Hingston. Royal Engineers.
Stoker PO. Thomas Squires, RN.
Revd. George S. Kewney. RN
2nd Lt. A. R. Taylor. RFC/RAF
Sgt. Paul De-Lappe Winter.
Rhodesian Native Regt.
Margret Carew. V. A. D.
Pte. Wallace Tozer. Devon's.
Pte. James White. Devon's.
Mary Rowlands. Q.M.A.A.C.
Stoker Richard Hard. RN.
Pte. Earnest Bishop. C. E. F
(Saskatchewan Regt.)

2. The Servicemen from South Brent who are not Commemorated on the St Petroc's Church War Memorial.

Pte. John Rowlands. R. G. A.
Pte. Fredrick Hall. Devon Regt
Chief Petty Officer Stoker Fred Joint RN.
Pte. Archie Joint Devon Regt,
Pte. Alfred John Goss DCLI.
Pte. Jarvis Lang. Devon Regt.

3. The list of Serviceman who are buried in South Brent grave yard and are not Commemorated on the War Memorial in St Petroc's Church.

Pte. Arthur Parsons. DCLI/Royal Defence Corp
Pte. Benjamin Cook. DCLI.

4. The list of Servicemen and Woman who were and raised in South Brent

Royal Navy

Chief Petty Officer Stoker Fred Joint RN.
Stoker PO. Thomas Squires, RN
Stoker Richard Hard. RN

British Army

Cpl. Henry Abbott. Anti. Air Craft Section.
Pte. Ernest Farleigh. Grenadier Guards
Pte. Fredrick Hall. 2nd/6th Battalion (Territorials) Devon's
L/Cpl. Bertie Hard. Machine Gun Corps
Pvt Archie Joint, 9th Devon Regt.
Pte. Jarvis Lang. 5th P.O.W. Battalion (Territorial) Devon's
Cpl. Henry Knott. Royal Garrison Artillery.
L/Cpl. Leonard H. Shillabeer. Devon's
Pte. George Smallridge, 9th (Service) Battalion, Devon's

Canadian Expeditionary Force

Pte. Earnest Bishop. C. E. F (Saskatchewan Regt.)

Queen Mary's Army Auxiliary Corps.

Mary Rowlands. Q.M.A.A.C.

NOTES

[1] The spelling in the local press at the time showed 'St Petrock's' with a 'K' in the spelling. This was dropped some when after the Great War for the present spelling 'St. Petroc's'.

Chapter Two

This chapter looks in some depth to the men and women who died during the Great War and whose names are inscribed on the War Memorial in St. Petroc's Church, South Brent. All their names are not in alphabetical order, they are in the order inscribed on the memorial.

S.Brent War Memorial
(Photo from Authors Collection.)

Herbert James Abbott
1896-1918

Herbert James Abbott was born in South Brent in the second quarter of 1896[1] to George and Martha Lucinda Abbott (nee Clancy) who lived at 2 Prospect Place, South Brent in 1901 when the census was taken. At the time they had three children, Fernley George, 7, Herbert James, 4 and Mary Clancy, 3. They also had an elder daughter, Elsie, not shown on the 1901 Brent census. George Abbott was employed by the Great Western Railway Company as a signalman.

The 1891 census shows an older sibling, Elsie, aged 5[2]. On the census for 1901, Elsie is living with her grandparents, John and Annie Clancy, in Plymouth and is employed as a dress maker.

It appears that Martha died sometime before 1909 as the census for 1911 shows that George was re-married to a Sylpha[3] and had been for two years, they were now living in Plymouth Road, South Brent. Fernley, the eldest son, was working as a porter for the G.W.R.[4], Herbert was a Grocers Clerk (boy), Mary and Nora Lucinda, born in 1904, were still at school.

It is not known when Herbert joined up but his number (1310) indicates it was either just before the war and was a possibly in the territorial force before becoming a regular soldier.

It is thought that he first joined the Devon's; he then transferred to the Royal Garrison Artillery. C. T. Atkinson (*The Devonshire Regiment 1914-1918)* does not list him as a member of the Devon's but that is not to say he was not in the regiment. His official number was changed to 168485, at some point and he was with the 152nd. Anti-Aircraft Section, Royal Garrison Artillery (R.G.A).

Herbert was serving in Palestine when he was killed in action on the 19th July 1918, aged 22. He is buried in the Jerusalem War Cemetery.

The land used for this cemetery was given by the people of Palestine to remember the fallen who died in the Great War.

The entry in the Commonwealth War Graves Commission register reads:

Herbert James Abbott
168485 Corporal
152nd Anti-Aircraft Section, Royal Garrison Artillery;
Formerly 1310 of the Devonshire Regiment. R. G. A.
Killed in action in Palestine 19 July 1918 aged 22.
Son of George Abbott, 6 Woodhaye Terrace, South Brent, grave V11. C. W. G.

Herbert has the inscription **'He died that we may live'** placed on his headstone. This inscription was requested by his father.

From his medal records, Herbert was awarded the Victory Medal and the British War Medals.

It is worth noting that Herbert's elder sister Elisa married Owen Edgar Burton at Totnes in 1905. He had joined the Royal Navy and is shown on the 1901 census as being on board HMS Vivid as an Engine Room Artificer in the West Indies.

During the war he was serving on board HMS Indefatigable at the battle of Jutland and was killed when his ship was sunk during this action. Owen's name is inscribed on the Plymouth Naval War Memorial. He left a wife, Elsie and a son.

NOTES

[1] Herbert James Abbott's birth, registered in Totnes, Vol. 5b. Page 172.

[2] Elsie married Owen Edgar Burton, 4th Quarter 1905, Totnes District, Vol. 5b. Page 360. They lived in Devonport. Elsie's husband, Owen trained as an apprentice turner with the GWR. at the Swindon railway works. 1911 census he is still with the Navy, based in Devonport and married for five years. Elsie died in 1963, aged 78 in Hendon Middlesex, District. Vol. 5e. Page 539.

[3] The birth and marriage details of Sophia are not known. Sophia died in September 1944, aged 78. Her death is registered in Plymouth, Vol. 5b. Page 312,

[4] Fernley George immigrated to Adelaide, Australia on the 12th April 1912, a 3rd class passenger, on the Orsova, belonging to the Orient Line. He returned to the UK before 1921 as he married Gladys Evans in the 3rd Quarter of 1921, in the district of Southwark, Surrey. Vol. 1d, Page 184. He died in 1938 in the Greenwich District, Vol.1d. Page 865.

Gilbert Thomas Butcher
1888-1917

Gilbert Thomas Butcher[1] was the fifth of seven children born to George Pallant[2] and Louisa[3], (nee Jones) Butcher. (Louisa Jones was George's cousin; she had lived with the family for several years as she had been orphaned).[4]

Their first son was John (Jack) William (1881)[5], followed by Charles Alfred[6] (1882), Louisa (1885)[7], Alice (1886), Gilbert (1888) Edward (Teddy) George[8], (1890) Carrie (1890) and Florence (1891) who died aged one month old. Caroline (Carrie)[9] was the only child to be born in South Brent.

The 1911 census has details of all the children born to George and Louisa, in total there were eight, only seven survived into adulthood.

The 1891 census also shows a domestic servant, Ellen Collins, aged 15 from Totnes working for them.

In her book, '*A Sporting Century*'[10], Ann Pallant mentions her grandfather, George Pallant Butcher, she states that George was a member of a Victorian Athlete and member of the London Athletics Club, at the same time as W. G. Grace, both being about 18 years old. George was a very accomplished athlete and had built up a reputation as a National athlete. It is no wonder that Edward, Jack, and Charles were all good sportsman, as we will see later.

He [George] started business in an Advertising Agency. In 1890, George moved his family from London to Aish Villa, South Brent. He was a frequent visitor to the area with its walking and the sea nearby. All the children (except Edward) attended the village school until the age of 10 when they all went on to be educated at King Edward VI Grammar School (Kevigs)[11] in Totnes. The children walked to the railway station to catch the train to school in Totnes daily and in all weathers. The walk to the station is about a mile from home and then a further half mile to school.

The family spent a lot of time by the sea and on the moors, their mother Louisa would take all the children as well as any local children by train to Kingsbridge then by ferry to Salcombe and then to South Sands for the day. They would take all their food and embrace the outdoor life. The family also kept a pony, for use as a pack horse, carrying their picnics and associated rugs and sports gear for moorland walks and games.

Edward (Teddy) left Kevigs in 1905 as Head Boy and held the 'Best Boy for Work and Play' prize. He then went on to the senior level of rugby, playing for South Brent. In 1905 all four brothers were in the South Brent rugby team and played

Plymouth Albion on Boxing Day that year. The score at the end of the game was Brent 46 points, of which the Butcher brothers scored 36, winning the match. One commentator at the match said: "*If Brent had eleven other chaps like they Butchers, they would lick New Zealander*"

Edward, (Teddy) Gilbert's elder brother went on to play for Plymouth Albion and was capped for Devon in 1908 aged 19. All four of the Butcher boys played cricket for South Brent, until 1907 when work commitments kept them away from Brent.

Gilbert had gone to work with WD and HO Wills, Tobacco Company at the age of sixteen and was working in London. He kept up his sport by taking part in the Imperial Tobacco Companies annual sports at Crystal Palace. The following tribute to Gilbert appeared in the national newspapers:

"*The Imperial Tobacco Companies annual sports took place today at the Crystal Palace. One of the principal events was the half mile for Mr Lambert's silver cup, which has to be won three times. Last year Gilbert Butcher, son of Mr G. P. Butcher of South Brent, a well-known sporting gentleman, who has won distinction on the cricket field, won it. There was stubborn opposition, but young Butcher was equal to the occasion, sprinted away from the half distance and won easily by a hundred yards in a time of 2min. 17sec.*"

Gilbert went on to win the race for a third year "*hands down*". His father said after the race that: "*Gilbert was a splendid sprinter and athlete*".

In 1909, Gilbert was at the Shepherd's Bush stadium in front of a crowd of fifteen thousand spectators, amongst them was the Princess Royal, Mayors and dignitaries from Devon and Cornwall, all were seated near the Royal Box. Gilbert won his heats in the 440 yard sprint and in the final came second.

The Imperial Tobacco Company sports event of 1910 saw him win the 300yard and 440 yard sprints from scratch and in July 1911 at the Coronation meeting winning the 300 yard and quarter mile events.

War was now about to start for Gilbert's younger brother, Edward Butcher, he was invited to join the '*Sportsman Battalion*' of the Northampton Regiment on the invitation of Edgar Mobs, the England and Barbarian rugby player. This battalion was formed on the 7th September 1914, with Edward enlisting on the 14th. His rank was a private soldier; he was aged 25 at the time. By February 1915 he had been promoted to a Corporal and was commissioned on 10 March 1915. In July 1915 Edward was sent on a Lewis gun course at Aldershot and spent the war in charge of gun crews. He survived the war, having been wounded twice, and left the army in March 1919 as a Captain. Due to injuries sustained during the war he was awarded a disability pension.

Gilbert's younger sister, Carrie went to a London Hospital and trained as a Volunteer Aid Detachment (V.A.D) nurse. It was whilst she was on a troop/hospital ship sailing to Malta she met her future husband, Dr John Portelli. After the war Carrie married John and they moved to Malaya where they lived and worked.

Gilbert was married to Catherine Kitty Blanch Stewart[12] (26) in Islington, London, in February 1914[13]. The marriage produced two children, Gilbert Herbert Stewart Butcher (1916-2000) and a daughter, Margaret.

In 1909 Gilbert joined the 15th (County of London) Battalion, (Prince of Wales Own Civil Service Rifles) part of the 4th London Brigade Territorial Reserve

When war broke out Gilbert was commissioned into the 4th Battalion (Extra Reserve) The Prince of Wales, North Staffordshire Regiment in September 1915 and was sent for training in Guernsey. His unit was sent to Marske in October 1916 and further moved to Saltburn in March 1917. In June 1917, the regiment moved to Westerner and was to come under the orders of the 200th Brigade, 67th Division, arriving in France in October 1917.

The problem with this information is that Gilbert never joined the 200th brigade. He must have been attached or posted to another unit some time before June 1917 as it is known that he was in France when he died on the 11th June 1917.

Gilbert is buried at Railway Dugouts Burial Ground, sometimes referred to by the troops as Transport Farm Cemetery. He is buried in section VII, row 12 of the cemetery in 1917.

In 1917 there were advanced dressing stations placed in the dugouts and at the farm. There is a good possibility that Gilbert was wounded and sent to the advance dressing station here and died of wounds and was buried.

Probate after Gilbert's death was granted to wife who was residing at Aish Villa, he left the sum of £206.00

There was a long article written on his death in what is thought to have been the Western Morning News of the day and copied to the Totnes and Mid Devon News.

One paragraph reads:

"A well-known Devon Athlete,
We regret to announce the death of Second Lt. Gilbert T Butcher, North Stafford's Regt. who was killed in action on June 11th? (1917) Left wife and son of 6 months old".[14]

There was also an extract from a letter sent to his widow, dated June 19th also published:

'I am writing to offer you my own and other officers and men of the battalion, our deepest sympathy. Your husband's loss is a very real one to us; he was always so steady and reliable under all circumstances and had done very good work. At the same time he was extremely popular with the other officers.

A.S.Conway, Major North Staffs. Regt.'[15]

After the war, Gilbert's widow applied to the war office for his war medals. He was awarded the Victory and British War Medals. They were sent to Mrs Moor, South Street, South Molton, Devon. Catherine had re-married in 1919.

There is reference on the KEVIC's war memorial to *E. G. Butcher, Lt.* Edward Gilbert Butcher, was the younger brother of Gilbert, who survived the Great War. It was Lt. Gilbert Thomas Butcher who died in June 1917.

NOTES

1 Gilbert Thomas Butcher was born in the registration district of Lambeth London, Vol. 4d. Page, 481.

2 George Pallant Butcher was born in the 1st quarter of 1846, his birth was registered in Lambeth London, Vol. 4, Page 2790, George married Louisa Jones, 29th October 1879 at St Marys Lambeth. He was aged 32, Louisa 24. George's occupation is shown as a Book Publisher. He died on the 28th October 1928 and his death is registered at Totnes, Vol. 5b, Page, 236. Probate was granted to his widow, Louisa. The value was £846 7/-. His residence is given as Aish-Villa, South Brent, Devon.

3 Louisa was born about 1855 in the parish of St Martins In-the-Field, London.

4 Anne Pallant; *A Sporting Century 1863-1963, Athletics- Rigby- Cricket.* Penwell Ltd, Callington, Cornwall, 1997. pp83.

5 Married Phyllis Annis Docking, (1899-1988) in 1924 at Croydon London.

6 Married Alice Annie Trinn, (1884-1967) in July 1908 at Kingston on Thames.

7 It appears that in 1911, Louisa was employed as a school teacher in the Sarisbury area of Hampshire, (near Southampton). She was a border at Locks Heath, near Fareham, Hampshire. She married Thomas Richards, the marriage was registered in Totnes in the 3rd quarter of 1912, Vol. 5b, Page 380. During the war she re-

mained in Aish Villa with her parents, her husband was an officer on the Western front. He was gassed but survived the war. He was never well for the rest of his life.

8 Married Nellie Orial Pugh-Jones (1895-1977)

9 Carrie married John Portelli at The Church of our Lady, Buckfast; the marriage was registered in Totnes District, Vol. 5b. Page 231. He died on the 15th June 1966, aged 73, (Newton Abbot District, Vol. 7a. Page 564) Probate granted to her son Dr John Edward Portilly, £5398. The marriage index uses the spelling Portelli, on the death certificate it is Portelly. The name change spelling occurred between 1929 and 1934.

10 Anne Pallant: A Sporting Century 1863-1963. Pp3

11 KEVIGS refers to King Edward VI. Grammer School. The name remained until the 1960 when it became a comprehensive School.

12 Catherine was born on the 18th Jan 1882

13 The marriage was registered in the Islington District of London, Vol. 1b. Page 233. In 1914. In 1919, Carrie re-married and became Mrs Fred Moor. (1883-1964) She died in Honiton March 1978, aged 96.

14 Totnes and Mid Devon News, 23rd June 1917

15 Totnes and Mid Devon News, 23rd June 1917

CHAPTER TWO

Jasper Carew
1894-1914

Jasper Carew

Jasper Carew was the eldest son of The Rev William Henry[1] and Maude Elizabeth Carew, born in Rattery, Devon in 1894[2] , Jasper also had an elder brother, Peter[3] and a younger sister, Margaret[4]. In the 1901 census he is described as a scholar aged seven. All the family lived at 9, Powderham, in the civil parish of East Teignmouth, Devon.

Jasper and his sister were educated by a governess by the name of Marrinia Griffin. In 1908, when he was aged 13, Jasper was a pupil at Blundell's School, Tiverton, where he remained until the summer of 1912. Whilst he was at Blundell's where he was a member of the school football team and narrowly missing out on obtaining his first colours.

In 1912 he left Blundell's and joined the Royal Military Academy,

Sandhurst as an Army Cadet. He completed his training and left in 1913. On leaving Sandhurst he received his army commission in 1914 and was sent straight to France.

His first commission on leaving Sandhurst was the 1st Battalion, the (Princess of Wales' Own) West Yorkshire Regiment.

The 1st Battalion was stationed in Litchfield in August 1914 and was part of the 18th Brigade, 6th Division. On the 7th August they transferred to Dunfermline, then six days later to Cambridge. The unit remained in Cambridge until early September then left for France, landing at St Nazaire on the 10th September 1914. This was the first division to relieve the B.E.F at Aisne.

Jasper saw action in France in the battle of Aisne[5], (12th September – 15th September) but sadly on 14th October 1914 he was killed. Captain Welshman[6] his company commander wrote to his mother two days later, he writes[7]:

"Dear Mrs Carew,
No doubtless you will have heard ere this reaches its destination of the sad death of your son in action on the 14th inst. As he was commanding one of the platoons of my company and was within five yards of me when he was hit, I wanted to let you have a hurried line to offer my sympathy and regret. My company advanced against the Germans at about 2.30pm: we developed against them and, outflanking their position, drove them from isolated farms and houses. At about 4pm I went forwards to see what was

going on and saw Germans in small numbers advancing. I called forwards your son with his platoon; we fixed bayonets and, charging, drove them off with some loss. A German maxim then opened fire at about 500 yards knocking out a few men; in silencing the maxim your son was hit by more than one bullet in the head and he was killed immediately. I don't think he even knew he was hit, it was quite instantaneous. He was a very brave boy. The previous day he and I lay side by side for three hours under heavy rifle and shrapnel fire and he never flinched. The men were very fond of him and I feel him a personal as well as military loss."[8]

The Officer Commanding the battalion also wrote to Jasper's mother with a resume of his army life whilst in France, he says:

"I am sure you will know, without my expressing it, how we all share and sympathies in your great loss. He was beloved by everyone – always cheery and bright under all circumstances, and we have had some trying ones. A most promising officer, absolutely fearless and he had done so well. He fell while gallantly leading his platoon in an advance guard action between Tout Verrier and Le Verrier near Hazebrouck. It was quite instantaneous, and he suffered no pain whatever and never moved."[9]

Lt. Jasper Carew was the first soldier from South Brent to be killed in action.

News of the death of Lt. Jasper Carew was published in the Totnes and Mid Devon News on the 31st October 1914, under the heading:

'Rattery'

Rattery heard last week of the death of Mr J. Carew, killed in action. The deceased was a 2nd. Lt. Yorkshire Regt. He was the youngest son of the late Reverend R.W. Carew who for 29 years was the vicar of that parish. Much sympathy was felt for Mrs Carew.[10]

There were two articles in the Totnes and mid Devon News on the week ending 7th November 1914 issue, the first under the headline:

South Brent

A large number of people attended South Brent Church on Monday afternoon on the occasion of the memorial service of the late Sub Lt J. Carew, youngest son of Rev. Carew (Deceased) and Mrs H. Carew of Airlea, South Brent. The deceased joined the army about 9 months ago and was killed in action on 12th. October 1914. The Rev. H. Speare-Cole and Reverend C. Parry-Keene (Dean Prior) officiated.

The other smaller article was more of a notice, the heading read:

Devon Officer Killed in Action

2nd Lt. Jasper Carew, West Yorkshire Regiment who was killed in action was the youngest son of the late Rev Henry Carew and Mrs Carew of Airlea, South Brent and joined the army in January of this year.[11]

Jasper is buried in 'Y' Farm Military Cemetery; plot N 13, near the Great Cross[12]. He is also remembered on the Rattery War Memorial at the entrance to the church in the village and on two locally produced memorials within the Church. One lists all the men of the village who enlisted.

Rattery Church Memorial to all the men and women who went to war and never returned. (Photos Author.)

Rattery War Memorial.

Blundell's School also a large memorial to all of the pupils of the school who died during the Great War.

Blundell's School War Memorial

Also on the memorial at Blundell's is the name 'CHG. Carew,' (Coventry George Warrington) Major, 7th Battalion Dorset Regiment. Killed in Action 20th November 1916.He has no known grave and is commemorated on the Theipval Memorial.

2nd Lt. Jasper Carew was posthumously awarded the British War and Victory Medals, his mother applied for his 1914 star in February 1918. In her correspondence with the army authorities she gives her address as, *'14 Westbrook, Pensilva Crescent, Exeter.'* On the medal records there is an old address of *'Airlea, South Brent, Devon,'* crossed out. There is also another old address on this record; it is *'Marley House, South Brent, Devon'.*

NOTES

[1] Died on the 14th December 1901, aged 56, Newton Abbot District, Vol.5b. Page, 68. Probate granted May 1902.

[2] Jasper Carew was born in the 3rd Quarter 1894, Totnes District, Vol.5b, Page, 177.

[3] Peter Fitzwilliam Carew married Joyce Fortescue, in the 2nd quarter 1919, Newton Abbot Devon, Vol. 5b. Page, 343. Peter died aged 66 in Cannes, France on the 31st March 1954. Probate granted in July 1955. Joyce was the daughter of The Honourable Arthur Fortescue, Kinson, Dorset. She died September 1974 aged 82.

[4] See Margret Carew, V.A.D. record.

[5] See Field Marshall Sir John French's dispatch dated 8th October 1914.

[6] Captain Welshman was himself killed ten days after writing this letter.

[7] This letter has not been corrected or altered grammatically.

[8] Courtesy of Blundell's School Archive.

[9] Ibid.

[10] Totnes and Mid Devon News, 31st Oct 1914.

[11] Totnes and Mid Devon News, 7th November 1914

[12] The cemetery was named after a nearby farm, called by the Army "Y" (or Wye) Farm. It was begun in March 1915 and used by units holding this sector until February 1918. At the Armistice it contained 335 burials, but it was then increased when graves were brought in from the battlefields south of Armentieres.

Ernest Farleigh
1889-1918

Ernest was the illegitimate son of Theresa Jane Farleigh, (1863-1959)[1] he was born in the first quarter of 1889. In the 1891 census he is shown living at The Bakers Shop, Fore Street, South Brent, with his mother and grandparents, William and Ella Farleigh. The household consisted of Theresa (27), Albert Waymouth[2], (22) baker, Albert Vanstone (16) baker's apprentice and Laura Soper (16) a servant.

Theresa married Robert Henry Gill (1867-1935) Postmaster, Grocer and Bakers Shop owner in 1891. The marriage was registered in the Totnes district. Ernest kept his mother's name of Farleigh throughout his life. According to the 1901 census, Theresa and Robert went on to have five children, one of which died as an infant. They were William Charles (1892-1941) Kathleen May (1897) Robert Henry (1902) and Eleanor Jane, (1905-1946)[3] There were four staff, a bakers apprentice, a telegraph boy, a domestic servant and telephonist/clerk; they all lived at number 3, Fore Street South Brent.

Ernest was educated in the village school and went on to Mutley Grammar School, Plymouth. On completing his education he joined the Western Daily Mercury[4], in the Plymouth office[5]. He was transferred to the Exeter office as a district reporter and wrote under the name of *'Pivot'* and was well known as a football critic. He also became the Hon. Secretary for the National Union of Journalists.

The 1911 census describes him as a Journalist aged 22, residing at 56 Portland Street, Exeter[6].

At the outbreak of war he went to enlist into the army with many others, but was rejected, probably on health grounds. This did not stop him as he resigned his position with the newspaper and took a position in the Territorial Records Office in Exeter. He remained in this post for eighteen months before being accepted as medically fit for active service. He then enlisted with the Grenadier Guards, (1st Battalion) and was sent for training at Chelsea and Caterham He married Edith Clara Towill, a tailor, of Newtown, Exeter, sometime during the second quarter of 1917, at Exeter.

Ernest's official number was 29961 and according to the records this is within the numerical category issued for those who enlisted between 13th June and 3rd July 1917[7].

It has not been possible to find out exactly what battles Ernest took part in, but it is known that the 1st Battalion of the Grenadier's were part of the 3rd Brigade which took part in one of the battles in the Somme area commencing in March 1918 and lasting until July of that year. There were several battles along the Somme line in which the 3rd Brigade were involved. They were: The Battle of St Quentin, 21st – 23rd March 1918, The First Battle of Bapaume, 24th – 25th March 1918, and The First Battle of Arras, 28th March 1918.

Ernest was killed on 5th April 1918, where exactly is not known but there was a small article printed in the Totnes paper on April 27th 1918.

Which read:

'Last week we recorded the death in action in France of Pte. E. Farleigh, Grenadier Guards, a former member of the editorial staff of this paper. His widow, who resides at Exeter, has received a letter from his Captain, who stated that her husband was instantaneously killed by a shell on the morning of the 5th Inst. And that a cross bearing his name has been positioned over his grave.'[8]

Ernest was buried in the Bucquoy Road Cemetery, in the Somme area of France. He is mentioned on the Commonwealth War Graves Commission register as being remembered in the *Special Memorial part of the cemetery.*[9]

The official document on the burial records show Ernest is believed to be buried in the cemetery but the actual grave is unknown. He lies with eight other soldiers of the Grenadier Guards.

His medal record shows very little except that he was awarded, posthumously the British War Medal and the Victory Medal.[10]

According to the War Graves Commission, Ernest's details state that his wife was Mrs Pope of '71, Portland Street Exeter'. It appears Edith re-married later, when details of the war dead were compiled in 1919/20.

From early April to August 1918, the cemetery was not used. In September and October, the 22nd, 30th and 33rd casualty clearing stations came to Boisleux-au-Mont and extended it. By the date of the armistice, it contained 1,166 burials but was greatly increased when the graves were brought in from the surrounding battlefields and from smaller cemeteries in the neighbourhood. It is very likely that Ernest was originally buried in the 'Bushes Cemetery' at Boisleux-St Marc, a small village just to the south. Here 17 soldiers of the 1st Grenadier Guards were buried from the battlefield in March and April 1918.

Ernest's younger brother, William Charles (1892-1941) would have been 21 at the start of the war and would have either enlisted or been called up. No details of any service has been found to date. The youngest brother, Robert would not have been old enough to serve until 1918.

NOTES

1 Died June 1959 age 96 in South Brent

2 The correct spelling of Albert's surname is not known as different census enumerators have spelt it 'Weymouth and Waymouth'

3 Eleanor married William Henry Shutt, (1907-1996) a Police Officer

4 The last *Western Daily Mercury*, number 20,459, was published on Monday January 31st 1921. From this date the paper incorporated with its former rival, *The Western Morning News*.

5 *The Western Daily Mercury* was a rival to *The Western Times*, both later to become *The Western Morning News*.

6 Ref. Vol. 5b, page 144, Exeter District

7 *Army Service Numbers,* 1881-1918: Grenadier Guards

8 *Totnes Times* 28th April 1918

9 Special Memorials are C.W.G.C. headstones which look the same as the usual ones but which do not sit over an actual grave. They have a superscription across the top denoting their purpose.

The list is as below:

Sp. Memorial. 1 Buried elsewhere in this cemetery

Sp. Memorial. 2 Believed to be buried in this cemetery

Sp. Memorial. 3 Buried near this spot.

Sp. Memorial. 4 Believed to be…

Sp. Memorial 5 This is known as a Kipling Memorial.

Sp. Memorial 6 Buried in… Cemetery (or Churchyard)

The Kipling Memorial headstone is so called because the quotation from the Apocrypha (Ecclesiasticus 44, verse 13) "THEIR GLORY SHALL NOT BE BLOTTED OUT" which appears on the headstone was chosen by Rudyard Kipling. These headstones commemorate casualties whose graves in a particular cemetery were destroyed or who were known to be buried in a particular cemetery but the exact whereabouts within the cemetery were not recorded.

10 National Archive Reference Number, WO372/7/15882. Medal Card.

Commander Cecil Halstead France-Hayhurst, 1875-1915

Cecil Halstead France-Hayhurst was born in Bostock Hall, Cheshire, the son of Charles Hosken (1832-1914) and Mary (nee Halstead, 1833 – 1877, age 34) France-Hayhurst, Cecil was born in 1875. He is shown on the 1881 census as the youngest of the five children living with his parents and four siblings, sisters Elizabeth (14) and Evelyn (11) and brothers Fredrick (1872-1915)[1] and William (1873-1947) at Bostock Hall, Cheshire. The census also shows the large household of twenty staff, including a governess for the children. Cecil's father was a Justice of the Peace and Lt. Colonel of the 14th Cheshire Militia.

Cecil joined the Royal Navy in 1890 as a Midshipman and is shown as such on the 1901 census. In July of 1890 he was serving on the battleship HMS Trafalgar. It took some time for him to be promoted from Midshipman to Sub. Lieutenant, but this happened in 1896 when he was drafted to HMS Crescent, a cruiser stationed in The West Indies and North America. He was further promoted to Lieutenant in 1898 and in October of that year he joined HMS Royal Arthur, (Flag Ship) again a cruiser but this time on the Australian station. The 1911 census shows him on board and in Sydney on the night of the census.

He remained on HMS Royal Arthur until May 1902 when he was again promoted, this time to Lt. Commander and was drafted to

HMS Fervent, as Captain. The Fervent was a Motor Torpedo Boat, (MTB) based in Portsmouth.

The Navy list of May and October 1903/4 respectively, shows him as having been drafted and promoted to Flag Officer to Vice Admiral Archibald Lucius Douglas[2], Commander in Chief North America and West Indies, on board HMS Aradine.

In November of 1903 he married Gertrude Isobel Douglas[3], the daughter of Vice Admiral Douglas, (his boss) in Halifax, Nova Scotia.

Gertrude was born in Japan when her father was stationed there and he has been credited with introducing football to the Japanese[4]. The wedding was recorded in the St John Daily Sun on Friday 20th. November 1903, with the headline:

"Marriage of second daughter of Vice Admiral Douglas"

After the wedding the couple honeymooned in Quebec, Montreal and Niagara before Cecil re-joined his ship at Bermuda[5].

Cecil returned to England and remained Flag Officer C. in C. Portsmouth. Promotion to Commander came in March 1907 and in October 1908 he was serving on board HMS Goliath, a battle ship stationed in the Mediterranean. He was the executive officer, second in command. *(Ironically Goliath appears later in this work when she is sunk.)* By July 1909 he is the Captain of HMS Goliath which was now back in England in the home fleet.

The 1912 Navy list confirms his appointment of Commander and in 1913 he becomes the executive officer of HMS Illustrious, a battleship with the third fleet based in Devonport.

On the outbreak of war Illustrious was one of the oldest and least well equipped ships in the navy. She was used as guard ship to the Grand Fleet and based in Loch Ewe, Scotland.

The November 1914 navy list confirms that Cecil was still the executive officer on HMS Illustrious. I have not been able to find out when he was drafted to HMS Patuca. (The next entry in the navy list is his obituary in April 1915.)

HMS Patuca was an armed merchant cruiser, pennant Number M77 which came into service on the 21st November 1914.

The ships log for 24th February 1915 states the "*Captain was taken to Hospital in Glasgow by ambulance.*" The ship then continued with her war duties,

Commander Cecil Halstead France-Hay Hurst, died in the 4th Scottish Military Hospital, Stobhill, Glasgow, cause of death, exposure whilst in the North Sea, on patrol

Cecil left a wife and two children. The Probate record shows that he lived in Avonwick, South Brent, and that Probate was granted on 3 June 1915 to his widow, Isobel, the amount was £1386 2/10d. Cecil has been commemorated on the South Brent and Davenham parish war memorials and is buried in St Wilfred Churchyard, Davenham, Cheshire.

12th June 1915, Totnes Times.

'CDr C.H. France-Hay Hurst, R.N. H.M.S Paula, of Avonwick who died at 4th Scottish General Military Hospital, Stobhill, Glasgow, on Feb 24, age 40. Left in settled property, of which gross value of £1386 2/10 of which £1261 12/6 is net personally.'

NOTES

1 Frederick Charles France-Hayhurst, born on 22 April 1872, served in the First World War as a Lieutenant Colonel of the Royal Welsh Fusiliers and was killed in action on 9 May 1915 at the battle of Auber's, near Ypres: he is buried at Cabaret-Rouge, Souchez, France

2 Sir Archibald Lucius Douglas, 1842 – 1913, G.C.B, G.C.V.O, Commander of the Legion of Honour, Order of the Rising Sun of Japan, Spanish Naval Order of Merit,

3 Canada Book 1820, Page 71, No.489

4 A full and very interesting history of Archibald L. Douglas can be seen on the Douglas Archive. www.douglashistory.co.uk/history/archibaldluciusdouglas.htm

5 Gertrude (16) was born in Japan to Constance (Ellen) Douglas (mother), father Ships commander serving with the Royal Navy at sea for the 1891 census. The family resided at Higher Velwell House, Rattery. Her younger sisters are shown as born in Dartington. The 1901 census shows her living in Kensington, London aged 26 with

Father, Archibald Lucius, (died March 1913) Admiral Royal Navy. With 2 sisters, May, (29) born in Plymouth and Constance (19) born in Totnes. 1911 census shows her married aged 26 with 2 children, girls, a 2 year old and a 1 month old, living in Guildford. It is worth noting that the children were born in Plymouth and South Brent. Gertrude Isobel re-married in second quarter 1919 at Kingsbridge to a Mr Thomas Arthur Champernowne, the son of Reverend Richard Champernowne, rector of Dartington, Devon Probate records show Thomas died in 19 July 1945, leaving £1521 3/10. Gertrude died in 29 November 1956 in Torquay, leaving £30,968 7/6. Both resided at The Vineyard, Totnes, Devon

CHAPTER TWO

Hugh Fanshawe Glanville
1884-1918

Hugh Fanshawe Glanville was the second child of Owen[1] (1848-1927) and Emily Glanville. He was born in Chobham, Surrey on the 24th November 1884 and Christened in Chobham Holy Trinity Church on the 25th December 1884, by his father.

The 1891 census shows him as a six year old residing at The Cedars, New Road, Teignmouth, Devon. His father was a Chaplin in Holy Orders. The family consisted of an elder brother, Percy (8)[2] and a sister Winifred (4)[3]. Also in the household was Mary Lovell, aged eighty, mother in law, Violet Lovell (9) a niece, both related to his father Owen, two child borders, aged eleven and eight, a cook and housekeeper.

The 1901 census shows Hugh a border at Plymouth and Mannameadian[4] College now known as Plymouth College. It is situated in Ford Park Road, Plymouth. Amongst its famous old pupils are Michael Foot, Labour leader (1980-83), Dawn French, comedian, Michael Ball, singer and actor and Tom Daley, Olympic Diver.

The Sandhurst military Academy records show that Hugh entered the academy in 1903 as a cadet and was commissioned in 1905. He next appears on the departing passenger list of the Port Royal, a passenger ship belonging to the Imperial Direct West Indian Mail Service Company Limited, destination Kingston, Jamaica. His is single and his occupation is described on the manifest as Lieutenant. The departure date is 12th February 1909.

The 1911 return of officers (census) for Bermuda and Jamaica show him as a lieutenant with the 1st Battalion West Indian Regiment, aged 26.

There is a reference to a H. F. Glanville arriving back into Plymouth on the 17th April 1912, on board the S. S. Tarquar, from Los Palma, Spain, travelling first class. This ship was owned by the British and African Steam Ship Navigation Company. It has been assumed that this is the same person. The chances are good as his Sandhurst Academy record show him as H.F. Glanville; this also ties up with his medal record which states that he disembarked May 1912. It also coincides with the granting of his aviators licence for flying a Bristol Bi-plane in 1912.

Hugh Granville

He trained at the Bristol Aircraft School, which was based at Brooklands Airfield, Hampshire. He was certified to pilot the Bristol Bi-plane on the 1st October 1912. Confirmation of his attaining his licence was reported in Flight Magazine of October 1912.

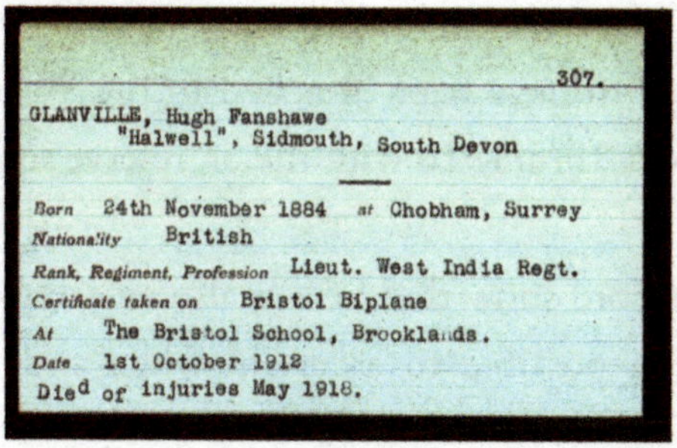
307.
GLANVILLE, Hugh Fanshawe
"Halwell", Sidmouth, South Devon

Born 24th November 1884 at Chobham, Surrey
Nationality British
Rank, Regiment, Profession Lieut. West India Regt.
Certificate taken on Bristol Biplane
At The Bristol School, Brooklands.
Date 1st October 1912
Died of injuries May 1918.

Royal Aero Club Certificate 307

What happened to Hugh after 1912 has been difficult to pin down. He is listed in the1913 Navy List of the Royal Flying Corps (RFC) as based at Farnbourgh as a Flying Officer, Rank Capt. He is also mentioned in The London Gazette listed for 1913, the entry reads:

Royal *Flying Corps. Military Wing. The under mentioned to be Flying Officers. Dated 17 Apr 1913. Lieutenant Hugh F Glanville, The West India Regiment.*

His medal record shows him going to France in August 1914, G.C. (General Command) 51st Wing, Royal Flying Corps. This is confirmed by Trevor Henshaw's, TSTB[5] that Hugh was serving with No. 5 Squadron, Royal Flying Corps[6].

Major Hugh Fanshawe Glanville was also the commander of No. 28 Squadron flying Sopwith Camels.[7]

He was shot down in Farman in May 1916 with No 16 squadron[8] and again being shot and injured in Voisin.

Hugh is believed to have been attached to the Warwick regiment from 10/2/1916 – 10/4/1916 with the 5th reserve squadron[9].

Hugh's service record show that he was also an army Chaplin but it has not yet been possible to ascertain when and where he was ordained.

He married Beatrice Gertrude Savory[10], the widow of the late Col. C. H. Savory in the 2nd quarter of 1918. They were married for 35 days before he died. The following notice of his marriage appeared in Flight magazine of May 1918.

"Captain HUGH FANSHAWE GLANVILLE, R. A. F., younger son of the Rev. O. F. Glanville, of South Brent, Devon, was married in London, by licence, on April 20th, to BEATRICE GERTRUDE, widow of Lionel C. H. SAVORY, of Dibden, Southampton".

The marriage was also recorded in the Totnes Times edition of the 4th May 1918[11].

Hugh was injured on the 23rd May 1918 in an accident involving his Avro 504, (number D44) during a training flight. He died later that day from his injuries[12]. Flight magazine carried the following article:

'Capt. Hugh Fanshawe Glanville, R.A.F., who died on May 24th at Gullane, East Lothian, as the result of an accident while flying on the previous day, was the younger son of the Rev. O.F. Glanville, South Brent, Devon. He joined the Royal Flying Corps in January, 1913, from the 1st West India Regiment in which he had served for eight years. He accompanied the British Expeditionary Force to France in August, 1914, as a member of the Royal Flying Corps. He had also seen service in Italy with the R.F.C.[13] *There was a student with him, Private. N.S Grant, he survived the accident'.*

The accident and death of Hugh was also reported in the Totnes Times a couple of weeks later on the 1st June 1918[14].

There was also an obituary in the Aero-Plane magazine[15],

"Glanville – Capt. Hugh Fanshawe Glanville, West Indian Regt. Attd. RAF has died from injuries sustained while flying on the Scottish east coast. He was 37 years of age, and son of the Rev. R.O.F. Glandville of South Brent, Devonshire. Capt. Glanville was born in 1884, and had his commission in the West Indian Regiment in January 1905. Transferring to the RFC in 1913, he reached the rank of Flt. Commander in September 1915."

(Note that the Totnes Times has Hugh as aged 33, Areo-Plane magazine Hugh is 37)

The record shows that Hugh's wife, Beatrice Gertrude Grenville, was granted probate, the sum of £422 12/2. Probate dated 1/8/1918.

Hugh's medal record shows that Mrs B. G Glanville made an application for the 1914 star due to her late husband, Capt. H. F. Glanville on the 24/11/1919. The reply address given to which Medal was to be sent was C/o Rev. O. J Glanville, 'Winsford' South Brent, Devon. The other medals awarded to Hugh were the British War Medal and the Victory Medal. He was also mentioned in Dispatches.

Captain Hugh Fanshawe Grenville is buried at Dirleton Parish Churchyard, East Lothian, Scotland. He is also named on the war memorial of Throwleigh, near Okhampton, Devon. It is not known why he is on their memorial. Enquiries with the village archivist have proved fruitless. He can find no records that Hugh was connected with the parish. He is also commemorated on the Teignmouth war memorial, on the sea front.

The family grave is inscribed:

'To the Glory of God and in ever loving memory of my husband Hugh Fanshawe Glanville, Captain WI Regiment and RAF, youngest son of the Rev O.F Glanville, South Brent Devonshire who after serving his

country in France and Italy during the Great War gave his life at West Fenton 24th May 1918 the result of an accident while flying age 33.'

Glanville, H.F. Lt. West Indian Regiment, Official No. 178/9 attached to Royal Flying Corps. Chaplin RFC.

Throwleigh War Memorial

The Teignmouth memorial

The inscription on the Teignmouth memorial reads:

'Captain Hugh Fanshawe Glanville of the 2nd Training Depot Station, the Royal Air Force. Son of the Rev. Owen Glanville and Emily Glanville of 'The Cedars', New Road, Teignmouth. Born in Chobham, Surrey in the December Quarter of 1884. Died, 24 May 1918 aged 34'. [16]

NOTES

1 1861 census shows Owen Glanville, age 13, Naval Cadet on the training ship Britannia in Plymouth sound.

2 Percy Glanville, born 2nd qtr. 1883, Kensington, and appears to have sailed to Australia as an apprentice. He is recorded again as qualified second mate for foreign ships, and later as Captain, with the Indian Marine Co. He next appears on the navy list of 1905 as a Lt. RN. He is not seen on the 1911 census for the UK, but could be on a ship's or dominion census. He died in Sept 1983, in Salisbury.

3 Winifred shown on 1901 census age 14, was a border at Clergy's Daughters School, Great George Street, Bristol. On the 1911 census Winifred is aged 24, living with her parents in Sidmouth. There is a grand-daughter, Audrey Grenville; (1909-1999) aged 1 born in Honiton, Devon. Who her father was is not known. Winifred married Percy Luscombe in Canada, April 1911. She returned to the UK in October 1923.

4 The school was established in 1877 and in 1896 it bought out its old rival Man-amead School (founded in 1854), and was temporarily known as Plymouth and Mannameadian College (hence the surviving abbreviation PMC). The school's motto, *'Dat Deus Incrementum'* – (God Gives the Increase), is the same motto as that of Westminster School, Marlborough College and Tonbridge School. (Source, PMC web site)

5 Henshaw, T. *The Sky, Their Battlefield*: (TSTB) The Complete List of Allied Air Causalities from Enemy Action in WW1

[6] Formed at Farnborough on 26 July 1913 *(Lewis. P. Squadron Histories, 1912-1959, P.14)* and following the outbreak of the First World War deployed to France on 15 August, equipped with a variety of aircraft types to carry out reconnaissance for the BEF. They flew their first missions on 21 August and on the next day, an Avro 504 of 5 Squadron was the first British aircraft to be shot down, its crew of pilot Second Lieutenant Vincent Waterfall and navigator Lt Charles George Gordon Bayly being killed.

[7] No. 28 Squadron of the Royal Flying Corps was formed on 7 November 1915. Initially a training squadron it became a fighter squadron equipped with the Sopwith Camel. After the end of World War I, No. 28 was disbanded. It had claimed 136 victories.

[8] No. 16 Squadron is a flying squadron of the Royal Air Force. It formed in 1915 at Saint-Omer to carry out a mixture of offensive patrolling and reconnaissance and was disbanded in 1919 with the end of the First World War.

[9] The information is from a listing on the Warwickshire Regiment web site for WW1.

[10] In 1902 Gertrude married Lionel Cyril H. Savory in Hastings in 1912 was living at 119 Earls Court Rd. London; her Occupation in 1913 was an actress. Gertrude left the UK in Oct 1919 for Colombo, Ceylon. Beatrice died Jan 1950, in London. She lived at the Empress Club, Dover Street, London, but died at Barrington Hotel,

[11] Bexhill-on-Sea. Her estate amounted to £12,232 17/4d

[12] Source: Flight Global Archive, 2/5/1918

[13] Service record information from the National Archives.

[14] Source: Flight Magazine June, 13th 1918 Casualties section:

[15] Courtesy Totnes and Mid Devon Times.

[16] Article from The Aeroplane, 29/5/1918

[17] Photograph by Author.

Edwin P. M. Goss,
1884-1918

Pvt. Edwin P.M. Goss, who is shown on the St. Petroc's Church memorial has proved to be a problem in tracking him down. There is some confusion as to who he actually is. Looking at the records we find **Edmond Percy Mabin Goss and Edwin Goss.**

It is known that **Edmond Percy Mabin Goss** joined the Army on the 25th July 1915 when he would have been about 30 years old, enlisting at either Devonport[1] or Torquay into the 8th (Service) Battalion, the Devonshire Regiment. His service number was 10907.

The 8th Battalion was formed in Exeter as part of the first New Army (K1) and then moved to Rushmoor Camp, Aldershot to become part of the 14th. Division. They were then mobilised to France in July 1917 landing at La Havre and became part of the 20th. Brigade, 7th Division, fighting in various actions on the Western Front.

The battles fought by the 7th Division (before the 8th Devon's joined them) included Loos 1915, Albert, Brazentin, the attack on High Wood, and Delville Wood, the battle of Guillemont, all in 1916. During 1917, with the German retreat to the Hindenburg line, the Arras offensive started with the fighting at Polygon Wood leading to the 2nd Battle of Passchendaele.

On November 18th 1917, the 8th and 9th were moved to Italy, arriving at Legnago on the 22nd November. They were there to strengthen Italian resistance against the Austria-Hungarian forces. Actions included the crossing of the Piave and the Battle of Vittoria Veneto.

It was either in this battle or as a consequence of this action that **Edmond Percy Mabin Goss**, died, he was not killed in action. It is thought that he might have died of wounds received, as this cemetery was used by 9th 24th and 39th. However it is suspected that he died from disease[2] as Edmond's medal record state that he **'Died'** not 'Killed in Action' or 'Died of Wounds'.

Edmond is buried in the Montecchio Precalcino Communal Cemetery[3]; plot 5 Row D. Grave 3. The location is north of Vicenza, midway between Venice and Verona.

Residing in South Brent at the time was an **Edwin Goss**, he was the son of Isaac and Mary Goss of Rattery[4]. Edwin married Florence Mabel Full in June 1908, and is shown on the 1911 census as a journeyman Baker residing in Newton Abbot. **Edwin Goss** joined the Somerset Light Infantry, service number 37591. He was discharged to the "Z" list on the 4th October 1919. So this is not who is named on the memorial. This Edwin Goss died in 1957, aged 73 in Totnes.

Edwin had a nephew, **Alfred John Goss**[5], Private, 27323, he enlisted at Newton Abbot and served with the 7th Battalion, Duke of

Cornwall's Light Infantry which was attached to the 8th Devon Regt. Alfred was born in Rattery to William and Mary Goss (Isaac's brother) His name is commemorated on the Theipval Memorial[6] and also the Staverton War Memorial[7]. *(See page 222 for more information.)* The photo of Pvt Alfred John Goss is from the Totnes Image Bank archive.

Alfred John Goss

There was also a second **Alfred John Goss**, 15490, (no known relation) who resided at Millswood, South Brent, he was married to Evelyn Freeman, with whom he had two children. He was attested at Totnes in January 1915 and discharged from the army in February 1915, medically unfit for army service[8].

There is further confusion, *C. T. Atkinson*, in his written work on the Devonshire Regiment, shows **Edmond Percy Mabin Goss** as having died in France and Flanders on these dates. The War Graves Commission documents state that **E. P. Goss, Private, 10907, Devonshire Regiment**, died and is buried in Italy. **E. P. M. Goss,**

Pte. Is also commemorated on the Torquay War Memorial.

On the South Brent War Memorial in St Petroc's Church is the name '**Pte. Edwin P.M. Goss. Devon's'** His army medal record show his name as **Edmond Percy Mabin Goss** and that he was awarded the 1914 Star, The British Medal and Victor Medal.

The Devon Heritage site has the following description:

'10907 Private Edwin Goss of the 8th Battalion, the Devonshire Regiment. Son of the late Isaac Goss and Mary Goss of Rattery. Born in Rattery in the December Quarter of 1884. Died 7 October 1918 aged 33'.

The discrepancy in the names is understandable with so many men killed with similar sounding names. What is amazing is that the village parish council or any of the parishioners of the village never picked up on the fact that this man was not a Brent man and never resided in the village

Torquay War Memorial
(Photo Author)

NOTES

1 The Ancestry web site has Edmund enlisting in Torquay.

2 The reason for stating Edmund died is that the cemetery where he is buried was used by the 9th, 24th and 39th casualty clearing stations between April 1918 and February 1919.

3 He was buried in Plot 5, Row D, and Grave 3 at Montecchio Precalcino Communal Cemetery.

4 Isaac Goss was born in Rattery about 1839; he married Mary Grace March in the 4th quarter of 1860, in the Totnes District, Vol. 5b. Page 345. He died in the 1st quarter of 1900 in the Newton Abbot District, Vol. 5b. Page 110.Mary Grace March was born in Blackawton about 1841, Married to Isaac Goss in 1860 and died in the 4th quarter of 1915, aged 74, Newton Abbot District, Vol. 5b. Page 159.

5 Son of William Henry and Mary Goss, nee Full.

6 Pier face 6 B.

7 Private 27323, Alfred John Goss, 7th Battalion Duke of Cornwall's Light Infantry, Killed in action, 6th September 1916. Son of William Henry and Mary Grace Goss, residing at Mount Cottages, Staverton, Totnes, married to M.M.J. Goss, 6 Cistern Street, Totnes.

8 See Private, 15490 Alfred Goss, Devon Regiment.

Charles Herbert Gribble
1892-1917

Charles Herbert Gribble[1] was ten years younger than his brother, Henry Bennett Gribble. Like his brother Henry, Charles attended Harrow school[2].

Charles Herbert Gribble
Mr Tony Milton, Gribble Archive, Harrow Archive

The baptism record shows that Charles was christened on September 13th 1889 at St Mary's Church in the Parish of Wimbledon. His father's occupation is shown as Solicitor and the service was conducted by the Curate, Mr Williamson[3].

The 1891 census shows the family living at 3 Thornton Hill, Wimbledon[4], It is noted that only Harriet 4, Katherine 3, and Charles 1, with a household of four domestic staff were present on the census day.

The 1901 census shows that there are now five children of Henry and Sarah living in Wimbledon , Henry 20, Harriet 14[5], Katherine 13[6], Charles 11 and Rose 8[7]. The eldest son, Henry Bennett was working as an articled clerk for his father and the remainder of the children are still at school.

Charles primary education was at St Andrews School, Southborough, Kent before going on to Harrow Public School, like his father and older brother Henry. He was admitted to Harrow in the Christmas term of 1903 and his house master was a Mr Davidson.

The Harrow Admission Register also shows that Charles went to Trinity College Cambridge in 1907.

According to the Cambridge admissions register he matriculated in 1907, to study for a Bachelor of Arts in Classics and History. In his first examination in Classics (1909) he attained a first class pass, and in his third year he attained a second in special history, part 1 & 2. His tutor during part of his time at Cambridge was Mr James Dull, a Classics scholar[8].

In the 1911 census Charles was residing at 101 Great Russell Street, W1, in the parish of St Giles in the Fields. His age is 21 and he was employed as a Tutor. His actual occupation was as an Assistant School Master at a prep school. What subject he was teaching was probably classics, where he was teaching is not known.

The household he was residing at appears to be a boarding house as there were several other residents as well as the owner's family, with five domestic staff.

There is very little other information on Charles from 1911 until 1915. He was unable to enlist at the very start of the war as he was suffering from Tuberculosis.

Charles army record shows he volunteered for service when war broke out with the Inns Of Court Rifles, Officer Training Corps (OTC)[9] on 28th February 1915. The document confirms the family details already written, with his medical examination and signing up carried out on the 1st March 1915 at Berkhamsted[10].

In June 1914, Charles became engaged to Dorothy Milton but the wedding was put off as Charles was supporting his widowed mother and younger sister's. He heard that he was likely to be sent to the front in 1916 and he and Dorothy decided to marry on the 12th August (his birthday) of 1916[11], their daughter, Dorothy-Rose was born the following year[12].

The marriage of Lt. Gribble was reported on in the Totnes and Mid Devon News on 19th August 1916[13]. Under the headline:

'South Brent'

'Lieut. C.H. Gribble, The Buff's, youngest son of the late Mr H.F. Gribble and Mrs Gribble of Splatton, South Brent, has been married at Marylbourne Parish Church to Miss. D.P. Milton'.

Charles was commissioned into the Buffs Regiment[14] in 1915. He was then attached to the 1st Battalion, the Royal Guernsey Light Infantry[15] and took part in the 3rd phase of the battle of Cambrai as part of the 29th Division. This battle was in response to the German counter attack which started on the 30th November 1917 and continued until the 3rd December 1917.

It was in this battle that Lt. Charles Herbert Gribble was killed in action. He was killed instantly by a snipers bullet at Rues Vertes, near Mesnieres. At the time he was in-charge of a company when the battalion came under a bombardment and a barrage of fire[16].

The Totnes and Mid Devon News reported in December of his death. The article read:

'*Lieut. Charles Herbert Gribble, Buffs, attached to Royal Guernsey Light Infantry who was killed on November 30th; aged 28 was the youngest son of Mrs Gribble of Splatton South Brent. He was married in August 1916 to Dorothy Phyllis, daughter of Mr M.H. Milton of Sussex Place, Regents Park, London, and leaves an infant daughter*[17] '

Charles is commemorated on the Cambrai War Monument in France, The Chapel of Trinity Collage Cambridge, Harrow School war memorial, as well as St Petroc's Church War Memorial in South Brent His name is carved on the Cambrai East Memorial at Louveral with others from the Royal Guernsey Light Infantry soldiers, all with no known grave.

Trinity College War Memorial, Cambridge is inscribed with the following:

In memory of the men of this college who gave their lives in the war, MCMXIV-MCMXVIII. The names of the fallen are on the both walls of the chapel.

Charles is also remembered on the Harrow School War Memorial. The memorial is in four parts, a main cenotaph in the chapel, and three engraved wall plaques, each with the names of the fallen from the Great War. The inscription on the cenotaph reads:

'*In Memory of the Sons of Harrow who died in the Great War, MCMXIV-MCMXIX*'.

The inscriptions on each wall plaque read:

'Be strong and of good courage, be not afraid neither be thou dismayed.'
'Be thou faithful unto death and I will give thee a crown of life'.
'Remember those who died for freedom and honour and see you to it that they shall not be forgotten'

The names of all the fallen follow each quotation[18].

Charles medal record shows his regiment as the

'*East Kent's, attach. Guernsey Lt. Inf.*'

There is a note written on the medal record,

'*Mrs D.P. Layton-Bennett (re-married*[19] *returns form EF9, in respect of her late husband's medals.*

It is interesting to note that the probate records for Charles show that he left an estate of £218 6/4d to Rose, his sister and Henry his elder brother.

Charles also left his mark in a literary sense. He wrote and published a book in 1917 entitled *'Regimental Silhouettes''*. The forward was written by Sir L.H. Smith-Dorrien. This book is a caricature collection in pen of various military types such as the Chaplin, the Commanding Officer, MO. and the cockney batman. In his forward, Sir L.H. Smith-Dorrien makes the comment that *'the likeness of the pen silhouettes is very true to life'.* The book has been out of print for many years and a copy has not yet been seen or obtained.

On the 25th November 1934, Katherine Gribble, (his younger sister) wrote to the War Office in London, asking for confirmation that her brother Charles had been killed in France in 1917. Her letter said:

Sir,

I want to make some enquires about my brother Lt. Charles Herbert Gribble, 2/4th Buffs (East Kent), reported missing at Messines, Cambria, November 1917, later declared killed.

Could you tell me the right officer to whom I should address my enquiry?
Yours,
Katherine Gribble.

The reply from the War Office dated 11th December 1934 asks for the precise nature of her enquiry.

In her reply, Katherine asks if anything definite has been heard of him, was his ID disc found, and on what grounds the War Office believes he was killed.

Katherine's original letter and subsequent reply caused the War Office to open a police investigation into Charles to see if he was killed or had possible deserted.

The internal report from the Military Historical section of the War Office states that:

'The Battalion on the 39th November 1917 was defending the line of the St Quentin Canal in the vicinity of Masneres (Valencinnes C.5 1:100,00). This was the day of the German counter-attack in the battle of Cambrai, but beyond stating that no infantry attack developed on the battalion front, although there was considerable enemy artillery action, and giving the name of Lieut. Gribble as killed in action on the 30th, no further details of the action are given in the war diary.
Historical Section (Military Branch)
20th December 1934.[20]

The inquiry was concluded in January 1935 and the following reply sent to Katherine[21].

Madam,

With reference to your letter of the 25th November, and subsequent correspondence regarding the late Lieutenant Charles Herbert Gribble, 4th Battalion, East Kent Regiment, attached 1st (Service) Battalion, Royal Guernsey Light Infantry, I am directed to inform you that the records of the department show that this officer was officially reported to have been killed in action on 30th November 1917, while serving with the British Expeditionary Force (France and Flanders)

I am to state that this report was made by the Officer Commanding, 1st Battalion, Royal Guernsey Light Infantry, the unit which Lieutenant Gribble was serving, and to point out that such a report would not have been rendered unless very definite evidence of his fate had been forth coming at the time.

I am to add that, on 39th November 1917, the 1st Battalion of the Guernsey Light Infantry was in section on the line the St. Quentin Canal, in the vicinity of Mesnieres.

I am,
Madam,
Your Obedient Servant.
V. Bovenizer

It appears that Katherine was still grieving for her brother and looking for some form of closure of his death.

The Gribble Annuls, (Vol. 111) has an undated letter from Charles's sister, Rose to her mother. In it she states that Lathom (Charles batman[22]) was asked for the details of what went on in France, he was unable to say or could not recall them. Rose thought he would tell what happened in a few months' time, but what he did say was noted carefully by Rose.

'On the 30th they were told to advance into the open and there were German aeroplanes up very many of them so Charles told them on no account to fire as until they did so the aeroplanes could not tell how many troops they were. They were all lying down flat of course and someone on the left lost their head, I suppose, anyhow they fired and the aeroplanes knew by the direction of the flash they were British so they gave the range to the guns. Charles was in Tommy's uniform but he had his glasses across and he had to put his head up to give the men the range as they had started to firing and he just called it out and was shot through the heart. He just turned over with a little gasp and Lathom caught him but he was dead at once'

Lathom had also said Charles had instructed him to take the things from his pocket but he did not like to and tried to find Captain Chapman. The letter then goes on to talk about family matters.

Before Charles was killed he wrote several letters to his baby daughter, Dorothy-Rose, the last two were dated 12th October 1917. One of the letters was to be kept for Dorothy until her 15th birthday. Both letters can be found in the appendices.

(News was received from Lynette Gribble (Dorothy Rose's cousin) that Dorothy died peacefully at her nursing home near Newbury, on Wednesday 1st October 2014, aged 98.)

Appendix 1
Letters to Dorothy-Rose Gribble, born in July 1917, from her father, Lt. (Acting Captain) Charles Herbert Gribble.

B.E.F.
France
12th October (1917)

My Dear Dorothy Rose

Three weeks ago today I went on a little expedition and had to return alone on foot to the camp which was four miles away. I had a very poor map, on which most of the roads, being new, did not appear. So I had quite a job. Occasionally I found a large white notice board with arrows and names of places, none of which appeared on the map. At last I got into a lane which became muddier and muddier. Some way on I saw a board, larger than most, and felt sure that this must have on it some familiar to me. It had no such on it. But before I got close enough to read it. I sank too deep in the mud. I could not walk through it. So I had to walk round a wide circle through a wood, and even in that the mud was up to my calves. At last I emerged close enough to the board to read 'All traffic to go slowly up this road, Horses to walk'.

And there's a true story for you, and it shows that there is fun to be had out of most things. But can you tell me how anybody got to that spot to put a notice up?

I'm very sorry to hear that you've been wakeful one of nights lately. You mustn't do that because you keep mummy awake too and then things go wrong. I shan't acknowledge your salutes if you're a bad one, you know.

They have such funny little horses here. The bad people were here for a time and they broke everything most destructively and immensely. They broke the people's houses till they lay flat as a tumbled card house (Aunt Rose makes those for you) they collected tables and chairs in great piles as high as a Church, and burned them all. They ate the cherries and apples, and because they had tummy-aches they cut down the trees in a temper. They made great holes as deep as dungeons where little houses had been. They burnt the thatch roofs and knocked the other kind off, so that they lay tilted against ruined orchard walls. They strewed the glass of the green-houses broken over the roads, and beautiful iron gates they twisted into ugly shapes as themselves. Then the good people come, and so they ran away for rear of punishment and now the thistles and weeds hide the rose beds, and it is all desolate where the bad people were.

But the good people are going to make it right again. So they come to work and they live in little houses made of paper. And they take three dads to build a little house with white paper walls and a red paper roof, and they sleep there at night, dry and warm. But in the day they work to make their country right again. So that when you are old enough to come and see it, it will be as before, and we will climb to a high place and look over the country that rolls away all round up and down in long low waves. And it will all be covered in warm fields and villages: fields of corn and beet, and villages with clean courts and whitewashed stone walls, and here and there a fine house and gardens of roses, and roses and roses. But just at present it is dull and looks as if someone had dropped your Dartmoor here, and as if the fall has flattened all the hills, killed the heather and turned the streams muddy.

I hope you are behaving well while you are staying with Mrs Kewney,

Your loving Daddy.

Charles also wrote two other letters that day, one to his wife and another too his daughter, with the proviso that the letter to his daughter must not to be opened until **6th July 1932** on her 15th birthday.

12th October (1917)

My Darling,

Here is the letter I told you I would write for the little one's 15th Birthday. Don't tell her of it till then. And here is a list of books for her to read. It is a wet day and we have no work to do, so I thought l would use this opportunity. I've all-ready sent you one letter today, so I'll get right on with the list.

1-7 Fairy Stories. Peter Pan, Andrew Lang's Fairy Books.
8-9 Jungle Book, Just So Stories, Treasure Island, Tom Brown's School Days.
10-12 Westward Ho, Hereward the Wake, Heroes of Asqard, Fletcher and Kipling's History of England, Cranford.
13-14 A Tale of Two Cities, David Copperfield, Esmond, a Lame Dogs Diary.

I find I have taken so long over this, and the list is incomplete, that I must leave it and gradually make out a proper one, and make a long job of it.

Rather rainy now, but we are in very excellent shelter,
My Love to you, sweetheart,
Your Husband.

The letter written by Charles to his daughter, to be opened on her 15th birthday on the 6th July 1932.

4th The Buffs
Attd. 1st (S) Br R Guernsey L.I.
B.E.F.
France
12th October

My dear little daughter

This is a letter which I told your mother I would write, in case I might not have the chance of seeing you grow up to this birthday. Don't take it as a golden rule of conduct, or imagine that you will find here compressed into what is only a letter any amount of wisdom to carry you through life. You will have been surrounded by kind wise peoples who will have loved you and cared for you as they have done to your father. And you will never forget, in fits of temper which you will have like other people, that the kindest and wisest of them all is your mother. You have been already a great joy to both of us, and to your mother you have been an object of increasing care by night and day. Don't forget that, and don't forget that you are so near to her heart that it would be impossible for her to deal rashly with you, so accept what she says a considered judgement. And don't imagine her that her judgement is likely to err. I, who know her best, can tell you that is not the case, So listen to her,

The last time I saw my father before he died, he was giving me some advice about my life at Cambridge. Whilst I listened, I reflected that it was nearly fifty years old experience and probably of date. Of course, I

said nothing, but he ended by saying exactly what I was thinking and regretting that I would not care to profit by his experience. I did not, and now I know I was wrong. Don't make that mistake.

You will have known by now that the Christian faith is. Let your conduct be actuated not be fear of losing your soul, by sense of gratitude to our Lord. Learn to hate ugliness in all things, ugly pictures, ugly speeches and ugly actions; and learn to appreciate what is clean and lovely. Learn to control your temper. Be ashamed of losing it except in someone else's cause. And don't despise fools. Village idiots are often happy, and give happiness.

Don't think of what other people are thinking of you. But be sincere with yourself. Don't let yourself persuade yourself that the easy thing is right, and then rest on your judgement. Don't hanker after showy work, or seek to be useful I another sphere to that in which you are placed. If you are cheerful, unselfish, dear girl, you will radiate usefulness and fulfil the prayer that your Mother and I have always made, that we may always have the wisdom to bring you up for God and his world. Never be discouraged. Read 'A Christmas Sermon' by R. L. Stevenson.

Never be unnatural. Don't affect a difficult mood before acquaintances and strangers. And don't forget, my little daughter that you may have to take my place in caring for your mother. And you'll find she wants a lot of watching, or she does too much. And when we meet, I shall be so very pleased to see you.

Your Father.

Charles Herbert Gribble was killed in action on 30th November 1917, one month after he wrote these letters. His daughter, Dorothy Rose was four months old.

NOTES

1 Charles was born in the 3rd quarter of 1889, birth registered at Kingston, Surrey, Vol.2a. Page 316

2 The photograph of Charles is from the Gribble Archive, by permission of Miss Dorothy-Rose Gribble, Charles daughter. It is the same photograph used by Harrow School in their memorial book.

3 Baptism record of St. Mary's, Wimbledon, Ref. No. 2853/1/1.

4 Henry Edward Gribble married Sarah Katherine Bennett 12th August 1897, a distant cousin.

5 Harriett Emily, 14, born 23rd May 1886, died June 1971, Bromley Kent

6 Katherine May 13, born 10th May 1888, died Dec 1974, Winchester Hants.

7 There were two other sons, Jack and Tom, both died as children.

8 Information from Mr Adam Green, the Archivist at Trinity College Cambridge; from *The Admission Register and College Records*.

9 The modern history of the Regiment begins in 1859 with the formation of the 23rd Middlesex (Inns of Court) Rifle Volunteer Corps. They were nicknamed "The Devil's Own" by King George III at a Royal Review in Hyde Park and this name has stayed with the Regiment ever since. To this day the Devil's image appears on regimental insignia and badges, an image believed to be unique in the British Army.

10 *WO374/29305 National Archives.*

11 The marriage was in the 3rd quarter of 1916, registered in the Marylebone, Middlesex, district, Vol.1a. Page 1264.

12 *The Gribble Annals*, Vol. 111, by Dorothy-Rose Gribble.

13 *Totnes and Mid Devon News, 19 August 1916.*

14 The Buffs; (Royal East Kent Regiment, formally the 3rd Regiment of Foot. The name 'Buffs' was the nickname for the regiment dating from the time they wore soft leather coats in the 17th century. The name Buffs was officially given to the regiment in 1744.

15 The 1st (Service) Battalion was formed in 1916 by the Militia and named the Royal Guernsey Light Infantry. They moved to Bourne Park, near Canterbury in May 1917 and were under the orders of the 202nd Brigade, 67th Division. In Sep-

tember 1917 they left the 67th and landed at La Havre and came under the orders of the 86th Brigade, 29th Division in October 1917. They took part in the Battle of Cambrai in late November 1917.

16 *Harrow Memorial to the Fallen, Vol. VI, PXXX*

17 *Totnes and Mid Devon News, 29th December 1917.*

18 Courtesy of Harrow School.

19 Dorothy re-married in the 1st quarter of 1920 in the Pancras district, Middlesex, Vol. 1b, Page, 193. She married Kenneth A. Layton- Bennett, (1890-1947) Dorothy (1894-1974) died in Newbury Berkshire, aged 78.

20 *WO374/29305. National Achieves*

21 *WO374/29305. National Achieves*

22 Lathom was Charles batman, he taken prisoner during the Great War. He was devoted to Charles and became the butler for Dorothy after being released. Dorothy re-married after Charles death.

Henry Bennett Gribble
1880-1919

Henry Bennett Gribble was born[1] at The Ridgway, 6 Hillside, Wimbledon, Surrey to Henry Edward and Sarah Katherine nee Denterfield[2] he was their first son. The 1881 census shows the house hold also had a nurse, and two domestic servants, who both originated from the South West[3]. Henry's father was employed as a solicitor.

The 1891 census now has the family living at 3 Thornton Hill Wimbledon; there are three more children, Harriett Emily 4[4], Katherine May 3[5] and Charles Herbert 1year old[6]. There is a Beatrice Gribble living at the home, this is the sister of Henry (Snr).

Henry Bennett is not shown on any census for 1891, he would be about 10 at the time of the census. In the Harrow School Register for the Easter Term of 1894, Henry Bennett is shown as a new pupil with a Mr Davidson as his house master[7]. Whilst at Harrow Henry excelled in Cricket and played for the first eleven. He was, sadly, unable to play with the team at Lords due to illness that plagued him all his life.

Henry Bennett next appears on the 1901 census working for his father as an articled Clerk and living with his parents in Wimbledon. There has been another addition to the family, a daughter called Rose Marian 8[8]. There was also four domestic staff living within the house hold.

Henry left England for Canada in 1908, to open up a branch of the family legal business there. He sailed on the SS Canada, arriving at Montreal on the 27th August 1908. He is shown on the ships passenger manifest as married, his wife was named Harriett, aged 22. I have not been able to confirm this fact, and it could well be an administrative error on the part of the shipping company.

In Henry's letter to his mother, dated 29th June 1915, he tells of his acceptance into the Canadian Army as Trooper Gribble, No. H826 Squadron, C. 11th Overseas Battalion Canadian Mounted Rifles. He goes on to describe life in the army and how much he is enjoying it.[9]

Before Henry joined the Canadian military, he had done some army training and service with the Inns Of Court Rifles[10], also known as 'The Devils Own Yeomanry'[11] His Canadian attestation document states this and he served for three years in the '*Inns of Court Rifles*', and his occupation is shown as a Solicitor.

It is also interesting to note that his maternal status is declared as 'Single'. Which seems to confirm that there was an error on the ships manifest, Henry was not married and had placed his mother's name in the 'Next of Kin' box, with the address of 'Splatton' South Brent, Devon, England.

According to the Canadian Army records, Henry enlisted on the 25th June 1915 into the 11th Canadian Mounted Rifles[12], his number is now 116425, changed from either H826 to 11826 by the Canadian

Army. This is somewhat different to what he said in his letter to his mother and could be due to bad handwriting. Having said that it was not unusual for men to be issued with different official numbers.

The 11th mounted rifles joined the 2nd Canadian Mounted Rifles and were attached to the 8th Infantry Brigade, 3rd Division Canadian Expeditionary Force (C.E.F). They took part in all of the major battles on the Western Front. Like all of the Canadian units they were identified by the square coloured sleeve badges with various geometric symbols on the top[13]. In the case of the 2nd Mounted Division, the square was in 'French Grey' with a red half circle on the top.

Sleeve Badge

It is at this point that information on Henry is missing. There is nothing on his Army records to account for this. Charles, his younger brother, writing to their mother in February 1917[14], states that Henry should be in France but is in hospital in England and Charles is hoping to visit him soon.

Why Henry was hospitalised is not known for certain, he is not recorded as having been wounded in action, but he was known to have had a chronic chest condition as he had suffered from chest infections for many years. It is assumed this was why he was hospitalised in September 1917.

Charles replies to a letter from Henry stating that:

'It's a good thing in one way because there is no doubt you weren't fit to go to France'

This seems to confirm the fact that Henry was suffering from a chest infection, probably tuberculosis. Charles goes on to say that he has asked his mother to write to Uncle Cortney to fix something in the service in England for Henry and that he should apply to be kept in England for the time being.[15]

It is known that he was still in England in 1919, where he was stationed, or if he was still serving or discharged from service with the Canadians is not known yet.

Henry Bennett Gribble died at Splatton, aged 39, on the 19th November 1919 of Tuberculosis and is buried in South Brent Church yard. The burial service was carried out by A.W. Cranch & Co.[16] who supplied *'One best oak coffin lined and trimmed with brass fittings'*.

The invoice from A.W. Cranch is dated December 19th 1919. Attached to the ledger page is a newspaper cutting, it reads:

'Roll of Honour,

Gribble-Henry Bennett, 11th Canadian Mounted Rifles, dearly beloved eldest son of the late Henry G Gribble of 38 Bedford Row, WC and

Wimbledon, and of Mrs Gribble Splatton, South Brent, of Tuberculosis contracted during training' [17]

On the same page off the Cranch ledger is a fee to the Vicar for a granite block and fixings. This is dated October 9th 1920.

The Granite Stone Memorial to Henry Gribble in South Brent parish church yard (Photo: Author)

There seems to be a discrepancy in the date for which Henry died. The Canadian Army Roll of Honour states he died on the 19th November 1919, yet the granite memorial in the church yard has the date of 19th December 1919. Henry's death was registered at Totnes in December 1919.[18]

NOTES

[1] Henry Bennett was born 26th May 1880 according to his attestation form.

[2] Sarah was born in Plymouth about 1857.

[3] One was Hanna Cocker the other was Ellen Redford both from Totnes

[4] Born about 1887, Wimbledon, Surrey

[5] Born about 1888, Wimbledon, Surrey

[6] Born about 1890, Wimbledon, Surrey

[7] *Harrow Admissions Register, Internet Archives, University of Toronto.*

[8] Born about 1893, Wimbledon Surrey

[9] *Gribble Annuls 111, p82.*

[10] The modern history of the Regiment begins in 1859 with the formation of the 23rd Middlesex (Inns of Court) Rifle Volunteer Corps; it became the 14th Middlesex in 1889. The Regiment was attached, in its later years, to the Rifle Brigade and also formed part of the 2nd London Volunteer Brigade and the "Grey Brigade". In 1888 amounted infantry detachment was formed and became known as "B" (M.I.) Company. A contingent of 30 mounted infantry, 19 cyclists and 1 signaller joined the City Imperial Volunteers for service in South Africa during the Boer War. *(Source. The London Metropolitan Archives)*

[11] They were nicknamed "The Devil's Own" by King George III at a Royal Review in Hyde Park and this name has stayed with the Regiment ever since. To this day the Devil's image appears on regimental insignia and badges, an image believed to be unique in the British Army.

[12] The 11th was mobilised at Vancouver and recruited in British Columbia. They embarked for England from Halifax on board the Lapland on the 16th July 1916, arriving in England on the 25th July. There were 36 officers and 883 other ranks. The 11th were attached to the 4th Canadian Training Brigade and sent to British Columbian units in France. These were the 7th and 29th Battalions and the 2nd Canadian Mounted Rifles. The 11th and 172nd Battalions were amalgamated on 1st January 1917 and formed the 24th Canadian Reserve Battalion.

[13] The full story of the evolution of Canadian formation patches, or "Battle

Patches" is given in Clive Law's book "*Distinguishing Patches*" available from Service Publications.

14 *Gribble Annals P.98*

15 *Gribble Annuls p.83*

16 Ledger details courtesy of Mrs R. Cranch's Archive.

17 From an unknown News paper

18 Registered in the Totnes District Dec 1919, Vol. 5b, Page 232.

Bertie Charles Hard
Military Medal
1885-1917

Bertie Charles Hard came into this world in December 1895[1] at South Brent, the second born of Mary Ann Hard (Nee. Chapman from Ugborough)[2] and Charles Hard (1868-1925) they lived at 36 Church Street, South Brent in 1901. Bertie had other siblings, they were Matilda May, the eldest, Lily[3], Thomas Stanley[4] and Sydney Richard[5].

On the 1911 census Bertie was 15 and working as a Groom/ Gardener Domestic, living at Town Mills House, South Brent. There have also been some additions to the family since the last census, with Fredrick George, 10[6], Harold William, 6[7], and Norman James, 2[8].

Charles's occupation at the time of the 1911 census was Farm Labourer. It is interesting to note that Charles and Mary had in total eleven children of which three had died. Matilda[9] (19) had left the family fold and was now in domestic service for a Mr Dodd, baker and confectioner at 132, Union Street, Plymouth.

Before Bertie joined the army he was employed as a telegraph messenger at South Brent Post Office, the Post Master at the time was Mr Gill. (The step father of Pte. Ernest Farleigh, Grenadier Guards.)

According to Bertie's medal record, he enlisted on the 27th July 1915 when he became eligible by age. He first joined the Devonshire

Regiment with the number 14181, indicating he was one of Kitchener's new army, (K1). Sometime later he joined the Machine Gun Corps and was issued with the number 18268.

He was attached to the 20th Company Machine Gun Corps, which in turn was part of the 7th Division, 20th Brigade; this unit was formed in February 1916.

Bertie was awarded the Military Medal[10] for acts of gallantry and devotion to duty in the field whilst under fire; this award was announced in the London Gazette.

According to the Totnes Times of 14th July 1917, Bertie, who had been gassed some four months earlier and had been evacuated to Blofield military hospital near Norwich, where he died in June 1917. His death was not officially registered until September 1917.[11]

Family memorial stone
(Photo: Author)

Bertie Charles Hard was posthumously awarded the 1915 Star, The British War Medal and Victory medal. He is buried in the North East corner of the church yard of St Petroc's Church South Brent; a small family memorial stone marks his resting place.

NOTES

[1] Bertie Hard was born in the 3rd quarter 1895, Totnes District, Vol.5b Page 165.

[2] Mary Ann Chapman married Charles Hard 3rd quarter 1891, Plymouth District, Vol. 5b. Page, 504.

[3] Married William H. Shearman, 3rd quarter 1917, Plymouth District, Vol.5b Page 614, Died Plymouth, September 1966, Vol.5b. Page 646

[4] Thomas died in March 1926. Totnes District Vol. 5b

[5] Sydney died in June 1925, Totnes District Vol.5b

[6] Fredrick George Married Lillian Fields, 3rd qtr. 1924, in the Totnes district, he died in Newton Abbot, September 1978 age 76

[7] Harold William married Ethel M Andrews, 4th qtr. 1947, Totnes district. He died March 1973, in Newton Abbot, age 68

[8] Norman James Died in Newton Abbot, age 61, September 1970.

[9] Matilda married Mr Sydney Bullen in the 3rd qtr. 1914. (vol.5b p249) She died in Milton, Kent, March 1926.

[10] The Military Medal was instituted by a Royal Warrant on the 25th March 1916. It was to be awarded for 'Acts of Gallantry and devotion to Duty', performed by non-commissioned officers and men in the army in the field.

[11] Bertie's death was registered in the district of Blofield, Norwich, Vol. 4b. Page 200.

Pioneer Benjamin Hingston
1875 – ?

Benjamin Hingston was born on the 14th November 1875 to Arthur and Selina, nee Petheyjohns Hingston. His father was a carpenter working in the area. Arthur was born in Kingsbridge, Selina in South Brent. In 1861 they were living in Lower Aish, South Brent with their daughter, Mary who was five months old. In 1871, Mary was visiting in Modbury, and the family had grown by seven more children, five boys and two girls, ranging in age from 8 years to ten months.

The 1881 census has not been filled in completely so their place of residence is not shown and there are three more children, two girls and one boy.

The 1891 census lists the family as living at 1 Island Cottage, South Brent. The 1901 census has the family, now reduced to two daughters, living at number 10 Station Road.

Benjamin is proving to be very elusive as far as the census and military records go. He is not shown on the 1881 census when he would have been six years old. In the 1891 census he appears aged 16 and employed as a masons Labourer living in South Brent, then he disappears again. His siblings appear right up until 1911, the latest census dates.

As for military records, he does have two medal records which show that he enlisted on the 27th July 1915 and spent his time in Egypt. His age on entering the army would be about 40-41 years old. He was awarded the 1915 Star, The Victory Medal and the British medal.

The medal records also show his rank as a Pioneer in the Royal Engineers, which would be about right as he was a stone mason before the war. His official number was 343 on one record and 452047 on the other.

Crucially the medal record show he was transferred to "Z" reserve on the 16th September 1919. Therefore it is safe to assume that he survived the war and he had been placed on the reserve list.

The "Z" list comprises of men who survived the war and were discharged from the army with the proviso that if hostilities were to breakout again they would be recalled for duty.

Benjamin is not shown on the War Graves Commission lists as having died during or after the war.

There is a reference to Benjamin that has been found it is a small article in the Western Times of January 15th 1896.

"*Benjamin Hingston, Alfred Howe, John Shillabeer, Thomas Hannaford and James Hannaford, of South Brent, prosecuted by Mr Kingwell for trespass in search of Coney's at Great Aish, South Brent, on December 27th, were fined 10s each and costs".*

There is a Benjamin H. Hingston shown as marrying in Cardiff in the last quarter of 1919 to a Miss Annie Blake and also a reference on the Great Western Employment register a 'B. Hingston' as working at Newton Abbot Railway workshops in 1932. It is difficult to prove that these are the Benjamin from South Brent without further documentary evidence.

The South Brent web site with details of the war dead from the village has no details on Benjamin, showing "*Not yet confirmed*". The only thing that has been proved is that he originated from the village, served in the war and according to the medal records survived.

Reverend George Stanley Kewney
Bachelor of Arts
1874-1916

George Stanley Kewney was born to Stanley Kewney (1844-1892) and Annie Kewney, (1857-1881), nee. Halstead, on 30th May 1874, at Tynemouth, Northumberland. George Stanley Kewney first appears in the 1881 census as a scholar aged six, residing at 45, Percy Park, Tynemouth. His father's occupation was a solicitor's clerk at the borough magistrate's court in Norfolk (1881-1919)[1] .

The 1881 census describes George's father (Stanley) as a widower, which indicates that Annie, his wife, died between the censuses of period of 1871 – 1881. Annie is not shown on the 1881 census return.

At the time of the 1881 census there were three visitors at their home, Ann Kewney, their Grandmother, Gertrude and Blanch, both his aunts. There were also two domestic staff, a housemaid and cook. Stanley senior re-married in 1881 to Salina Foster, aged thirty five. The union produced two sons, detailed on the 1891 census as Alfred Lionel (8) and Harold (5).

Stanley, senior, died in 1892 and probate was granted to his widow, Salina. In 1931 Salina died aged eighty eight and leaves her estate to her two sons, Alfred and Harold[2].

The 1891 census shows George is now aged sixteen and a border at North Eastern County School, in the district of Barnard Castle, County Durham. He then went from here to Cambridge University, Pembroke College and matriculated in the Michaelmas term (October) of 1892.

George gained a Bachelor of Arts in Theology and was ordained a deacon at Newcastle-upon Tyne in 1895 and a priest in 1898 where he had his first post as Curate of Cambridge-on Tyne until 1900. He then joined the Royal Navy as a Chaplin and Naval Instructor.

In the last quarter of 1900 (19th July 1900) he was married to Lydia Cousins Stephens (1874-1907) at Hexham, Northumberland.[3] Her father was a ship owner in Newcastle upon Tyne. In 1901 she was staying with her uncle in Newcastle, also a ship owner.

In April 1900, George appears on the Navy list as a Chaplin, and again in that November as a Naval Instructor.

His first ship in the navy was HMS Caledonia (1901); from there he went to HMS Cambrian until 1904. HMS Cambrian was a cruiser in the South East Station of America. He joined HMS Irresistible, a battleship in the Mediterranean fleet in 1904 and HMS Emerald later that year.

The Navy List of 1905-9 shows him as Chaplin on HMS Commonwealth, a battleship with the Channel fleet, he remained on her until 1909. He also served as a naval instructor teaching navigation.

In 1907, his wife Lydia dies in Weymouth, aged thirty two, the reason is not known and there appear to be no children from this union[4].

From 1909 until 1911 he is Chaplin on HMS Dreadnought, Flag Ship to the Commander in Chief, Sir William H. May.

The marriage index for Christchurch, Hampshire for the 2nd quarter of 1910 shows him getting married to Margret Catherine Bain, aged twenty eight from Glasgow[5].

The 1911 census, for Bere Regis shows him as a visitor, age 36, married under one year, with wife, Catherine, age 28. He and his wife were staying at the Royal Oak Inn, this was a guest house or pub with accommodation.

1911 saw him drafted to HMS Cumberland, a training ship for cadets.

He was then moved to HMS Highflyer in 1913, a light cruiser, again a training ship but based in Devonport. She was re-commissioned at Chatham on 29th August 1913 and completed in Devonport on 4th September 1913. He is remained on board HMS Highflyer until 1915.

The passenger list for the SS Orita, owned by the Pacific Steam Ship Navigation Company, shows George returning to England from Calico, Peru, joining the ship at St Vincent in the West Indies, arriving at Liverpool on the 15th September 1915.

There is no information on when he joined HMS Queen Mary but as it is well known she was one of three ships in the First Battle Cruiser Squadron. The others vessels were HMS Princess Royal and HMS Tiger.

The official history of the destruction of the Queen Mary at the Battle of Jutland, (31st May 1916) was written by Sir John S. Corbett[6]. He [Corbett] writes:

At 4.10, being then eleven miles away abaft the beam of the Lion, he inclined inwards a couple of points, and as Admiral Beatty simultaneously altered still more to port to press his van, he was able at 4.17 to re-open fire at extreme range. To the Germans she must have been invisible, for the Derfflinger, mistaking the Princess Royal for the flagship, began firing on the next astern, which the *Seydlitz was also engaging. Thus the Queen Mary, from 15,800 to 14,500 yards, became the target of both these ships.*

For about five minutes she stood it gallantly. She was fighting splendidly. The Germans say full salvoes were coming from her with fabulous rapidity. Twice already she had been straddled by the Derfflinger, when at 4.26 a plunging salvo crashed upon her deck forward. In a moment there was a dazzling flash of red flame where the salvo fell, and then a much heavier explosion rent her amidships. Her bows plunged down, and as the Tiger and *New Zealand raced by her to port and starboard, her propellers were still slowly revolving high in the air. In another moment, as her two consorts were smothered in a shower of black debris, there was nothing of her left but a dark pillar of smoke rising stem like till it spread hundreds of feet high in the likeness of a vast palm tree.*

At 4:26 pm, a shell from Derfflinger struck Queen Mary detonating one or both of its forward magazines. The resulting explosion broke the battle cruiser in half near its foremast. A second shell from Derfflinger may have hit further aft. As the after part of the ship began to roll, it was rocked by a large explosion before sinking. Of Queen Mary's crew, 1,266 were lost while only twenty were rescued.[7]

It is thought that the anti-flash hatches between the gun turrets and the magazines were not shut as they should have been when '*closed up*' for action and one shell exploded near an open hatch allowing the blast to travel through the hatch and passage ways to the magazine, causing a catastrophic explosion destroying the ship and its crew.

The Rev. George Stanley Kewney was one of fifty seven officers and one thousand two hundred and nine men who perished with their ship. These men are remembered in their local Parish Church's and memorials, but also on the Naval Memorial on Plymouth Hoe.

George is also remembered and his name has been inscribed in the roll of honour at Barnard Castle School. Here there are two volumes on names that have been on a lectern with an inscribed traceries top, near the rear of the Chapel. The names of one hundred and forty one former pupils and four teachers are remembered. George Stanley Kewney was posthumously awarded the 1914 Star, the Victory and British War medals.

The probate records show he left £513 7/4d to his wife Catherine who at the time was living at Splatton Cottage, South Brent, Devon. Catherine passed away in June 1972 at Leighton Buzzard, aged eighty nine.

NOTES

1 On Henry's death in 1919, the probate record describes George as "Gentleman". Henry left his estate to George Halstead, Gentleman. It could be assumed that this was his mother's brother who was not present is on the census return of 1881.

2 Alfred marries Annie Philipson in 1912. He died 16th December 1959 aged 77. Harold marries in 1909 and dies in Bullingdon, Oxfordshire in 1974, aged eighty eight. Both boys from the second marriage were trained as engineers in the shipyard.

3 3rd Quarter 1900, Hexham Reg. District, Northumberland,Vol.10b, Page 561

4 Lydia Cousins Stephens born 1st quarter 1874, Newcastle, Northumberland.

5 1st Quarter 1907, Weymouth Dorset, Vol. 5a, Page 230

6 3rd Quarter 1910, Christchurch, Hampshire, Vol. 2b, Page 1447

7 Based on official documents by direction of the historical section of the committee of Imperial Defence in 1923,

8 Extract from the Official History, *"Naval Operations"*, Sir Julian S. Corbett, 1923. Vol. 1-5, Longmans Green & Co. London, Second Ed. 1938

Alfred Paul De-Lappe Winter
1889-1918

Alfred is not a Brent boy by birth; he originates from Somerset, in fact he was born in the first quarter of 1889, (29th January) with the birth being registered in Bedminster, Bristol, (Vol 5c, p690).

His father was William Alfred Winter; (1852-1931) was married to Constance, nee Whipple, and (1862-1945). According to the 1891 census Alfred was age 2 years and living at 69, Yatton Road, Clevedon, North Somerset with his siblings, Constance Mary aged 8, Kathleen Ada, 6, John 4 and William Arthur, seven months. Their father's occupation was a Sanitary Inspector.

In the 1901 census Alfred was 12 and was a visitor to the home of James Clapp in Yatton Road, Clevedon. The relationship between James and Alfred was is not known. The census also shows Alfred as 'De lap' Winter.

The Great Western Railway Records show Alfred employed as "*Lad Clerk*" number 6 in the passenger department of Totnes railway Station in 1905, age 16. He worked there until the 19th April 1907 when he resigned.

Alfred next appears on a ships passenger manifest on the 7th January 1911, when he sailed from Southampton on board the Union-Castle Mail Steamship line ship **Galeka,** destination Cape Town, South Africa.

The 1911 census shows Alfred's parents living at Shirlea, South Brent. His mother Constance was the village district nurse/midwife, and his father a farmer. Nurse Winter became the community nurse in the village as the Totnes Times reported in 1915 and 1916.

Arthur was mentioned in the Totnes and Mid Devon News on 24th October 1914, when he returned on leave from South Africa to visit South Brent. The article said:

"Amongst those from South Brent who have joined the army are Paul De lappe Winter was on his way here from South Africa on leave joined the Natal Light Horse, his brother William Arthur Winter will be joining the RFC."

Arthur was a member of the Natal Light Horse initially but his Army Records show him as a sergeant in the Rhodesian Native Regiment, later to become the Rhodesian African Rifles.

The information given on the Devon Memorial site is incorrect in almost every respect. The site states that:

"*Paul de Lappe Winter was born in Clapham in 1888. He was the son of Frederick and Ida Winter, both foreign nationals. His father was a foreign correspondent and consequently, the family made many moves around the world. Paul had gone from Cape Town to Rhodesia and joined the British South Africa Police which, in 1916, formed a Native Regiment comprising 54 Europeans and 456 native soldiers, under the command of Major Tomlinson.*"

It seems odd for such a mistake to have been made as the Totnes and Mid Devon News for October 1914, (above) contradicts the Devon Memorial Site Information. This is further borne out by the fact that Arthur's mother served the parish for some time as the District Nurse.

The Totnes and Mid Devon News printed the yearly report of the parish nurse (Mrs Winter) submitted to the parish council on at least two occasions. The first being report on 23rd March 1915;

"*A meeting and yearly report by the district Nurse Winter. Made 1693 visits and attended 23 births in the parish*"

Again in 16th March 1916, the headline read;

Annual meeting of the South Brent Nursing Association.
The report by the parish nurse, Nurse Winter, stated that in the past year it had been busy with 1705 home visits and 34 maternity cases. The meeting expressed their thanks to Nurse Winter. It was proposed that Nurse Winter be given a present. This would be discussed at a later date.

This last sentence suggests that Nurse Winter was due to leave the parish.

Sgt. Arthur Paul De Lappe Winter. No.1396 died on the 20 December 1918, aged 29. He is buried in Zomba Town Cemetery. Malawi. His grave number is 87. The War Commission Grave information states that he was the Son of William A. and Constance E. Winter, of Dovercourt, Dawlish, South Devon, England. Cause of death, pneumonia.

Richard Veale Hard
1901-1918

Richard appears on the 1901 census as a one month old baby, born on the 5th June of that year. He was the third child of John Scott[1] and Elizabeth Jane[2] nee Witt Hard[3]. The family lived at 45 Church Street, South Brent. The household consisted of John William Scott, aged 3 and Ada Elizabeth, 1 year old. John senior was employed as General Labourer.

The family had grown a lot since the 1901 census. By 1911 the family consisted of a further four children[4]. Kathleen Maude 7[5], Ethel Florence 5[6], Kate Rosina 3[7], and Alfred Henry, six months.[8]

John William (13)[9] had left the family home and was a servant at Wonston Farm working for Mr Alfred and Mrs Mary Sherwell, Ada[10] and Richard were still at the village school and living in Church Street. Richard's occupation before joining the Navy was a Horse Driver.[11]

Richard enlisted into the Royal Navy in June 1918 when he became 18. His service number was K/52211, with the rank of Stoker 2nd Class, based at HMS Vivid at Plymouth. (Now HMS Drake Naval Barracks, Plymouth)

Sadly he died in July 1918, aged 18 years old, about one month after joining up, at the Naval Barracks in Devonport.

He had contracted the Spanish Flu which was sweeping post war Britain. [12]

Richard is buried in St Petroc's churchyard with a Commonwealth War Grave headstone. Richard was never awarded any war service medals, and he was never married.

Richard's head stone, in St Petroc's Church. (Photo: Author)

NOTES

[1] John Scott Hard, 1871-1961, was born in the Totnes District Vol. 5b. Page 192. He died in 1961, aged 89, Totnes District, Vol. 5a, Page 1053.

[2] Elizabeth Jane Witt, 1876-1937. Born at Portsea Island, Hampshire, 3rd quarter 1875, Vol. 2b. Page 383. Died December 1937, aged 67, Plymouth District, Vol. 5v. Page 425.

[3] Elizabeth and John married in the 2nd quarter of 1897 in the Totnes District, Vol. 5b, Page 333

[4] The 1911 census of children, Kathleen Maude 7, Ethel Florence 5, Kate Rosina 3 and Alfred Henry six months.

[5] Kathleen Maud was born in the 3rd quarter of 1903, Totnes District, Vol. 5b. Page 151, she married William Mudge in 1922, registered in the Newton Abbot district, Vol.5b. Page, 350. Kathleen died in September 1955, Newton Abbot District, Vol. 7a, Page 700.

[6] Ethel Florence was born is the 4th quarter of 1905, her birth was registered at the Totnes District, Vol. 5b, Page 145. She married Thomas Scamp in the 3rd quarter of 1927, Newton Abbot District, Vol. 5b. Page 336, and died in June 1985, registered in the Plymouth District, Vol.21, Page 1747.

[7] Kate Rosanna was born in the 2nd quarter of 1908, Totnes District, Vol. 5b. Page 159. She married Leslie Hinds in the 4th Quarter of 1929, Totnes District, Vol. 5b. Page 411.

[8] Alfred Henry was born in the 4th quarter of 1910, Totnes District, Vol. 5b. Page 140. He married Kathleen Jones in the 4th quarter of 1940, Totnes District, Vol. 5b. Page 669, died in July 1989, aged 78, Newton Abbot District, Vol.21, Page 1440.

[9] John William Scott (1898-1966) married Dorothy Violet Scamp (1908-1969) in the 2nd quarter of 1928, Devonport District, Vol. 5b, Page 761.

[10] Ada Elizabeth (1899-1986) married William Sowden, 4th quarter 1919 at Totnes. Vol. 5b, Page 497. It appears that William died and Ada was re-married to Archibald Fare (1908-1974) in Plymouth during the 1st Quarter 1940. Vol. 5b, Page 1066.

[11] ADM 188/968/52211, National Archives.

[12] Richard's death was registered in East Stonehouse, Plymouth, Vol. 3b Page 338

Henry Richard Knott
1891-1917

Henry Knott was a Brent boy through and through. His father was Thomas Knott (1843-1918) and mother, Susan Penny Knott. The 1891 census first shows Henry as a baby of five months old. There are four other children, William 10, Alice 8[1] , Amey 6[2], and Albert 3.

In the 1901 census return, Henry was aged 10 and a scholar, living with his parents. His father, Thomas was a mason, journeyman, and with the family they all lived at Brent Mill. His brother, William, who was born in Paignton was employed as a sales assistant Albert, also born in Paignton and is shown as a being at school. Thurza Knott, aged 73, described as 'Sister in law', was also residing with the family.

The 1911 census gives Henry as being 20 years old and was employed as a Mill hand Washer; the family was still residing at Brent Mill. William was now employed as a Draper aged 40[3] and single. Albert is shown as a baker aged 23 and single.

The census also shows that there were five children in all, but the girls do not appear on the family 1901 census. Their names on the 1911 census have been crossed out and "*away*" marked. The younger one Amey was 25 years old, and Alice Mary, was aged 28. Both girls were listed as employed in domestic service. Thurza Knott is missing from the census and it is presumed she had died sometime between 1901 and 1911.

Henry applied to join the army and enlisted at Newton Abbot in 1915. On his application form for the army he is shown as a machinist aged 25 living at Clarence Cottage, South Brent. He signed on for service in November 1915 and the document was counter signed on the 18th November 1915. He states he is Single and gives his mother as his next of kin.

The service number allocated to him was 69715 and he had joined the Royal Garrison Artillery (R.G.A) as a gunner. His effective date of commencement in service was the 4th November 1915 when he was posted to the R.G.A. Depot.

21stDivision Insignia worn on the upper sleeve of the tunic.

The attestation document gives details of Henry's measurements, marriage status and children (if applicable) as well as his Statement of Service at the base of the document. The writing is difficult so the details have been transcribed.

In January 1916 he was posted to 32 Company at Culver, Sandown on the Isle of Wight, as a gunner.

On the 23rd January he was sent overseas, (France) with his company. On the 4th March 1916 he was again posted to the 2nd army for further training in the field.

Later in March (26th) he was posted to the 21st Medium Mortar (Z) Battery, R.G.A.[4] This battery was attached to the 21st Division, Kitchener's third army[5].

The third from last entry on his army record reads "Killed in Action, B.E.F France, 6/10/17". The next entry says

"*Body Exhumed for Re-Burial, Hooge Crater 2 miles*".[6]

Henry saw action in the Battle of Albert, Brazentin Ridge, Flers-Courcelette, Morvil and Le Transloy, all phases of the Battle of the Somme in 1916. In 1917 he would have been involved in the Battles of Arras.

The Totnes and Mid Devon News published two articles on Henry[7]. The first was printed on the 20th October 1917 informing the Knott family of Henry's death just after returning to France from leave. (Note the paper said Henry is in the Motor Transport Section, this should read Trench Mortar Section.)

South Brent,

'*Mr and Mrs Knott of Brent Mill, South Brent, have been notified that their son, Cpl. Henry Knott, Truck Motor Section, has been killed in action. After being home on leave. He left for France exactly a week previously.*'[8]

'*At South Brent Parish Church on a recent Sunday, pulpit references to the deceased were made by the Vicar and the "Dead March" was played at each service.*'[9]

The Totnes and Mid Devon News published a further article one week later:

'The parents of Henry Knott, 'a Bomber' with a Trench Mortar Battery, who reside at South Brent, also received a letter from Lieut. Robertson of the Battery, in which he says:

"I deeply regret to have to inform you that your son, Corpl. Knott, was killed in action on Oct. 5th. The officers and men of his battery all send their sympathy. He was very popular with everyone and an extremely brave man. I feel the loss personally as he was with me as soon as he joined the battery and I found him so thoughly reliable that I promoted him to Corporal. It may afford you some consolation in your sorrow to know that he suffered no pain as he was killed instantly. I am arranging his funeral and am having a cross made to put over his grave."

An official letter dated 19th March 1918 was sent from the War Office London to the Officer in Charge of the R.G.A, Dover, giving instructions on the disposal of Cpl. Henry Knott's effects and medals. All his possessions are to be sent to Henry's mother, Mrs Susan Knott, Brent Mill Cottage, South Brent, Devonshire.

These instructions were carried out by the Officer Commanding in Dover. The official letter sent to Mrs Knott, (with a receipt attached) was sent on the 25th March 1918. Henry's effects were signed for by his mother on the 28th March 1918. The sum total of Henry's effects received by Mrs Knott consisted of '**One Photo**', not much to remember her youngest son by.

In May 1919 another official letter arrived requesting information of the issue of the scroll and plaque (The Death Penny) for Henry, in accordance to the King's wishes. The form has to be signed by the member of the family named and certified as correct by a minister or magistrate. Then it has to be returned so that the issue of these items can be completed. Corporal Henry Richard Knott was finally laid to rest at Hooge Crater Cemetery, Belgium.

Mrs Knott also had to sign for Henry's medals when they were issued in 1921

In an article published in The Totnes and Mid Devon News of the 21st October 1917, informing of the death of Henry, reference is made to 'Mr & Mrs Knott', yet on the official documents sent by the Army later were addressed to Mrs Knott.

Thomas Knott had been killed in December 1918 in an accident at the Brent Mill. The Totnes and Mid Devon News reported on the inquest of Thomas's death. The headline read:

"*Fatality at South Brent*

It appears that the clothing of Thomas caught in the wheel and he was carried around the wheel several times. When the machinery was stopped, Thomas had sustained serious injuries. His work mate was knocked unconscious. Police Sergeant Beer obtained a stretcher from the school and Thomas was sent to the South Devon and East Cornwall hospital, where he died the next day. The other man on regaining consciousness then walked home without further treatment. The factory inspector was satisfied that there was no negligence and a verdict of accidental death was recorded.'

Mrs Knott applied to the magistrate's court in January 1919 for administration of compensation paid for the death of her husband. This was reported in the Totnes paper on the 1st February 1919. It read:

South Brent.

At Totnes County Court on Tuesday, Mrs Knott made an application for the administration of £211 14s 2d, paid into the court as compensation for the death of her husband, Thomas Knott, who met with a fatal accident at South Brent. Applicant desired the money to be invested to the best advantage, so that 8s weekly should be paid to her, – The Judge agreed and directed £11 14s 2d to be paid to her and the remainder to be invested in War Bonds.

NOTES

1 Alice is aged 16 on the 1901 census and is in service in the village to a Mr Hoskins, a widower aged 80 and retired newspaper agent, residing in Station Road, South Brent. On the 1911 census, Alice is still in domestic service but she has left the area. Her work is in Richmond Hill, Surrey. She is in the employ of William and Margret Morrison, (65 and 64) of independent means, with three other domestic staff.

2 In 1901, Amey is 15 and now in domestic service at Nolan Park Lodge, South Brent working for Sibyl Hoskings, (71) a retired grocer. The 1911 census shows

Amey as a domestic working in Nolan Park, South Brent. Her employers now are Mr and Mrs Carter. He is 85 and his wife 77.

[3] In 1920 William was the Verger in St Petroc's Church.

[4] By March 1916, most Divisions had three *Medium* Batteries, designated X, Y and Z. For example, in the 24th Division they would be X.24,Y.24 and Z.24

[5] The 21st Division was established in September 1914, as part of Army Order 388 authorising Kitchener's Third New Army, K3

[6] The cemetery was first begun by the Burial Officer of the 7th Division in October 1917. There were originally 76 war graves, Rows, A-D of plot number one. The cemetery was increased in size after the armistice when the dead from the Zillebeke, Zantvoorde and Gheluvelt battlefields were brought in. Several small cemeteries were also closed down and the bodies re-located to Hooge. The crater was made by a mine sprung by the 3rd Division. On 30 July.

[7] Articles courtesy of the *Totnes and Mid Devon Times, Published 20th October 1917.*

[8] Ibid

[9] Ibid

Colin Cecil Langford
1888-1918

Colin Cecil Langford was the youngest of three children born to William Thomas[1] and Mabel Fanny, nee Gilliat Langford[2]. William and Mable married in Chorley Wood, Hertfordshire on the 10th August 1880, William was aged 33 and Mabel 19.

Colin Cecil Langford
Picture Harrow School Archive

Colin was born in Paddington, London on the 24th May 1888[3] and baptised on the 27th June at St Stephen's Church, Kensington, London. The family resided at 28 Beechin Place London.

In the 1891, census, Colin was aged two and he had an elder brother, Edward Gilliat 9[4], and sister, Noel Mable 5[5]. Colin's father is described as a barrister in the city of London. The household also had six staff living in, a cook, parlour maid, under maid, nurse, general domestic and a coachman/groom.

The 1901 census for the family does not include Colin; he is a border at Rottingdean School and shown on the school census aged 12. After completing his primary education he went to Harrow School in Middlesex, arriving in the Easter term of 1902 and leaving in 1904[6]. He enlisted with the Royal Field Artillery in 1908[7] and obtained his commission in 1909 whilst with the Isle of Wight Militia, based at Sandown.

The 1911 census has his name on two returns, the first one for '*Officers, Warrant Officers, Rank and File Soldiers form*', on this form he is shown as a Lieutenant aged 23 but **absent** on the census night. The other census form is the one completed by his father. Here he is entered on the census as being at home in Plymouth. Colin's home address is shown as 'Bank of England Place, Plymouth'.

Prior to the outbreak of war, his unit were on their annual camp on Salisbury Plain. Orders from the War Office instructing the division to take precautionary measures in the event of war. On the 3rd August the Brigade moved into positions to defend the ports, with the divisional headquarters being established in Exeter.

On the 5th August 1914, all units were mobilised for full time war service and the division re-organised on Salisbury Plain with the Headquarters located at Tidworth.

In September 1914, India agreed to send 32 British and 20 Indian regular army battalions to Europe in exchange for 43 territorial force battalions. This allowed Kitchener to send the well trained regular army to France as part of the initial B.E.F, with the Territorial units being destined for India, in exchange for the regulars returning.

The territorial, units (with Colin Langford) assembled at Southampton on the 9th October 1914. There were three additional units, the 4th, 5th and 6th Devonshire regiment[9].

They all sailed to India via Malta and the Suez Canal, landing at Karachi on the 9th November 1914. On arrival at Karachi all the units came under the Command of the 3rd (Lahore) Divisional Area at Ferozepore, (4th Devon's) Multan Divisional Area were joined by the 5th Devon's and the Divisional Area at Lahore, the 6th Devon's. Whilst in India, Colin was in command of an artillery battery with the acting rank of Major.

Colin remained in India until December 1917 when he was sent to the Western Front, France. He was then attached to 'A' Battery 295th, 43rd Wessex Division, Royal Field Artillery where he received his promotion to Major. This promotion was published in the Supplement to the London Gazette on 2nd May 1918. His promotion date was 2nd April 1918.[10]

Colin left A' Battery on the 2nd April to command 'D' Battery of the 295th Brigade, R F A.

The War Diary for the 295th Battery states that they landed at Le-Havre on the 14th March 1917. The battery moved the guns up to Eterprigny on the 25th to be ready for action and were in position by 1:30pm on the 26th.

On the 28th March, batteries A, B, and D, moved forward to Catelet and set up in the old brick works. D battery was then moved again to Porcupine Wood, map reference Q.1.a.2.9. Nothing much is recorded for D battery until February 1918.

From the war diary it appears that D battery came under heavy fire at 5:15am on the 21st February 1918 at Varacourt. This lasted for four hours, the fire coming from the east.

There is a notation at the end of the diary which says *"Great Gallantry was shown by the ranks during this engagement especially the 21st."* This entry was dated 28th February 1918.

Major Colin Cecil Langford was wounded on the on the 9th April and died later of his wounds. The action he was involved in was at Douch Valley near Bapaune, seven days after being promoted to Major.

Captain O'Brian, 'A' Battery 295 Brigade R.F.A wrote to Colin's parents, he informed them that:

'His loss is very deeply felt out here by all who knew him, both officers and men. He was a first class gunner and the best of friends: everywhere you go you hear praise of him. It was exactly the same in India, his battery did better than any other in camp and the men were so keen to do him credit, they would work like niggers for him'.[11]

The Totnes and Mid Devon News announced the death of Colin Langford in the issue of the 20th April 1918. It read:

'Capt. C.C.L. Langford, R.F.A. of Charford Manor, Avonwick, has died of wounds received in action'.[12]

Further on in the same issue of the paper an obituary was written:

'Avonwick Officer Killed'.

Captain C. C. Langford, R.F.A., was the, younger son of Mr and Mrs W.T. Langford, of Charford Manor, Avonwick. He was wounded in action on April 8th, and died the same day. Born in 1888 he was educated at Harrow and received a commission in the R.F.A. in 1909, passing through the Isle of Wight Artillery Militia. He went out at once to India where he served until 1917 when he was ordered home. For some time before leaving he was in command of his battery as acting Major. Early last December he went to the front, and at the time of his death was in command of a Field Artillery Battery, and was to have been promoted Major in a few days. His elder brother, Lieut. Col. E.G. Langford, D.S.O, R.F.A., has been at the front since August 1914 and is now in charge of F.A. Brigade[13].

Colin was buried at the Gezaincourt Communal Cemetery Extension[14] a small village south west of the town of Doullens[15]. He is buried in plot 11, row K 12. The War Graves Commission grave index at Gezaincourt reads:

"Died of wounds received at Adinfer wood, 9 April 1918, age 29"

He is also remembered on the '*Harrow School Memorial to the Fallen*', in Middlesex as well as St Petroc's Church, South Brent.

Probate for his estate was granted on the 2nd August 1918, he left £750 17/6d to his mother Mabel who was residing at Charford Manor, Avonwick, Devon

There is a notation on Colin's medal record stating that his father had applied to the War Office for his medals on the 25th May 1921. Major Colin Langford was awarded the Victory medal and the British War Medal.

NOTES

1 William Langford was born in India in 1847 and died in March 1922. His death was registered in the Totnes District, Vol. 5b, Page 303. Probate was granted to his widow, Mabel, his effects amounted to £237 16/11f.

2 Mabel Langford was born in Paddington, London in about 1866 and died at Plympton in June 1950, Ref. Vol. 7a. Page 707. Probate was granted in August 1950 in London to Edward Gilliat Langford, retired Lt. Colonel. The effects amounted to £2273 2/-

[3] Colin's birth was registered in the 2nd qtr. 1888, Kensington District, London, Vol.1a, Page170.

[4] Edward Gilliat was born in the 3rd quarter of 1881, (3rd. July 1881) registered in the Kensington District, Vol. 1a. Page 105. And christened in Chorley Wood on the 7th August 1881. He was married to Winifred Lettice Adair on the 26th June 1915 in Chelsea Holy Trinity Church. Edward died in the New Forest district, Hampshire, aged 96, in March 1976. Ref. Vol; 20. Page 0414.

[5] Noel was born on the 30th December 1885 and registered in January 1886 in the Kensington District, Vol.1a. Page 178. She was christened on the 31st January 1886 at Chorley Wood. She died in June 1978, aged 92 in the Plymouth District, Ref. Vol.21, Page 1732. Her married name was Mac Worth. It is not known when she married but is shown on the 1911 census as such. Noel arrived back into England from Sydney in 1929.

[6] The Harrow School Register, 1800-1911.

[7] Photograph courtesy of Harrow School Archive.

[8] Kitchener actually sent the Wessex Division, minus the ammunition columns, Royal Engineers, Royal Army Medical Corp, and the Hampshire Heavy Battery, R.G.A.

[9] The 4th Devon's were raised in August 1914 in Exeter, the 5th Devon's were raised in Millbay, Plymouth, and the 6th Devon's were raised at Barnstable. All were part of the Devon and Cornwall Brigade, Wessex Division.

[10] SUPPLEMENT TO THE LONDON GAZETTE, 2 MAY, 1918.
The under mentioned to be actg. Maj. whilst comdg. Batts.: —Capt. C. C. Langford, R.F.A 2nd Apr.1918. (spelling and grammar as published)

[11] From a Letter written to Mr and Mrs Langford, By Captain O Brian, R.F.A. April 1918.

[12] Articles by curtsey of the Totnes and Mid Devon News 20th April 1918.

[13] Totnes and Mid Devon News 20th April 1918.

[14] The Extension was opened in March 1916 and used until March 1917, and again from March to October 1918. In most cases, the burials here were carried out from casualty clearing stations and, in June to August 1918, from the 3rd Canadian Stationary Hospital.

[15] The village is situated between the main road from Doullens and Abbeville

Raymond Richard H Newman
1892-1915

Raymond Richard Newman has proved very elusive to track down as he first appears on the census of 1901. His birth was in Tyringham and is registered in the district of Newport Pagnall, Buckinghamshire in the first quarter of 1892. (Vol. 3a. Page 771) On the 1901 census he is aged 9 and living with his grandmother, Harriet Hext Newman, aged 62, from Staverton and her daughter, Kate aged 21, at Firleigh, South Brent. Kate was born in Diptford in 1880. Her father was a farmer of 130 acres employing men to work the land, at Downstow, South Brent and she is one of six children[1].

One thing that stands out is that by 1901 Thomas Newman, grandfather of Raymond, is still alive and in Diptford with his eldest son Ernest running the farm, whilst Harriet is in Brent with Kate and Raymond. It appears that the village web site is wrong as Harriet was not a widow as stated[2].

This is borne out by the death of Harriet on 7th May 1910, in Bristol. Her probate record shows that her estate was worth £139. 3/- shillings and was left to her husband Thomas Newman and her eldest daughter Annie Elizabeth Coleridge (nee Newman)

Raymond Richard Newman enlisted into the Duke of Cornwall's Light Infantry (DCLI) 2nd Battalion, official number 9169, at Totnes before the war.

He next appears on the 1911 census for the parish of Gravesend, Kent and he is a resident at Gravesend Barracks, which includes the military hospital. It lists him as a member of the 1st Duke of Cornwall's Light Infantry, aged 20. The regiment moved on to Tidworth Barracks, on Salisbury Plain, in 1911 then on to Curragh, Ireland in 1913. His [Raymond's] official number, '9169' indicates that he joined the army before the 12th February 1909[3], just after his 18th birthday, making him a regular soldier. It would appear that Raymond joined the army for a military career, rather than go farming. There is another reason for this move, as it appears from the census records that he was illegitimate, hence living with his grandmother.

The start of the Great War, the 1st DCLI was one of the first West Country regiments to be sent to France. The DCLI were stationed in Ireland at the time and were now becoming part of the B.E.F, the 14th Brigade, and 5th Division, which landed at La Havre in 15th August 1914.

The regiment, including Raymond took part in the opening attacks in the Battle of Neuve Chapelle, (10th March – 22nd April 1915). He was not killed in the main advance on Neuve Chapelle but the smaller 'sub-battle' of St Eloi (14th–15th March 1915) three days later. The official date of Raymond's death is recorded as the 14th March 1915.

Raymond Richard H. Newman has no known grave so is immortalised on the Menin Gate Memorial at Ypres on panel 20.

The Menin Gate, Ypres, Belgium.
(Photo: Author's collection)

Raymond's medal record shows that he was posthumously awarded the British War Medal, the Victory Medal and the 1914 Star.

NOTES

[1] The youngest daughter, Harriet S. Newman is shown in the 1901 census as residence in the 'County Lunatic Asylum' Exminster, Exeter, aged 20, no occupation.

[2] From South Brent Village Web Site;

Raymond Richard Newman of the 2nd Battalion, the Duke of Cornwall's Light Infantry. Born in Tyningham, Bucks in the June Quarter of 1892 but brought up by his widowed grandmother, Harriet Hext Newman who ran a boarding house in South Brent. He was a regular soldier who was killed in action 14 March 1915 aged 22'

[3] RegimentialNumbers;*www.hargreavemawson.demon.co.uk/DCLINos.html*

Private Joseph Oliver
1895 – 1915

Joseph was the second son of William Henry and Elizabeth Jane Oliver. William was born in Helston and Elizabeth hails from Camborne.

Their first born appears to be William in 1894 and Joseph arrived in 1895, the 1911 census shows that Henry and Elizabeth have been married for eighteen years and they have had six children with only two surviving, William Henry and Joseph. Both boys were born in Illogan, Cornwall.

The 1901 census shows them both as seven and six years old respectfully. Their father's occupation is unreadable but he appears again in the 1911 census as the resident engineer at Didworthy Sanatorium, South Brent. The census also shows Joseph as an odd job boy employed at Didworthy Sanatorium, aged 16. William, his elder brother has moved on and it is known he had joined the Royal Navy in October of 1913[1].

It is not known when Joseph enlisted but he was employed as a driver in the Army Service Corps. His official number, (T1/3302) the prefix "T1" indicating he was driver of horses and wagon and his company, 102 was formed on the 28th August 1914 and disbanded on the 21st June 1919. The unit served on the Western Front with the 14th Division.

Joseph died of injuries sustained by a kick from a horse on the 12th January 1915. When Joseph died he had been in the army for less than six months.

The Totnes and Mid Devon News carried the following article in the issue of 23rd. January 1915.

Sad death of South Brent Volunteer

Driver Joseph Oliver, son of Mr Oliver, engineer at Didworthy Sanatorium, Didworthy, South Brent, was the first to volunteer for service when the war broke out. He was attached to the Army Service Corp at Aldershot and died a few days ago from a kick in the breast by a horse. Great sympathy for the parents whose other son was in the navy.

Joseph's death was recorded in Hartley Witney, registration district in the first quarter of 1915, (Vol. 2 page 334) he was aged 19. He is buried in the Aldershot Military Cemetery, grave AF 1791.

NOTES

1 William Henry Oliver joined HMS Vivid 17th October 1913 as a Stoker. Official Number, K20931. He left the service on the 5th April 1927. William died in Newton Abbot aged 85 in March 1979. (Vol. 21, Page 1805)

John Ernest Salter
1897–1917

John Hambling Salter[1] married Mary Elizabeth Reeves[2] at St Mathew's church, Hammersmith, London on the 15th April 1896.[3]

John Ernest Salter, their eldest son, was born in the 4th quarter of 1896 in West Kensington, London[4], and baptised on the 3rd January 1897, at St. Mathew's Church, West Kensington.

On the 1901 census he was aged 4 and living with his parents in Hammersmith, London. His father's occupation is described as a tailor and there were two other adults living at the address, Susan Reeves 25, sister in law and employed as a domestic servant and George Wake, employed as a tailor.

By the time the 1911 census was taken the family was living in Church Street, South Brent. (There is a notation in the Kelly's Directory, 1910.[5] '*Salter, John Henry, Tailor Church Street, South Brent*'.)

John Ernest Salter is described as a '*Scholar*' on the 1911 census. It is worth noting that there had been four additional children born since the previous (1901) census, George Edward[6] 10, Vera Rosina[7] 6, Horace[8] 5, and Agnes Joyce[9] 3, all were born in South Brent.

The 1911 census states that Mary had given birth to six children of which five survived.

John was an active member of the village; he was employed by his father in the family tailoring business, a member of the Church Sunday School and Choir.

John Ernest Salter
Picture from Mrs M. Eales collection

When war broke out in 1914, John would have been only 17 too young to have enlisted. He would have to wait until Jan 1915 when he would be 18 and eligible. He did finally enlist and did so in Torquay.

This picture of John[10] in his uniform is a bit of a quandary. He is shown wearing what appears to be a Devon Regimental cap badge, and he has been attributed to the Devon Regiment on the War Memorial in St Petroc's Church, but there is no record of him in the Regimental History of the Devon's[11] or with the Commonwealth War Graves Commission information. Here he is listed as a gunner of the 1st/1st Warwick Battery; Royal Horse Artillery.

John's army records were destroyed in the second war by a direct hit on the repository in London where all first war army records were stored. Some were saved but the majority were lost. As a result we are not able to accurately follow John's period of action in France and can only look at the date of his death to work out what action he might have been involved in.

John is recorded as being a gunner with the 1st/1st, this battery being involved in the 3rd Battle of Ypres. They took part in the opening barrage on the 25/26th July 1917. During this action, John's battery took many casualties.

By the end of July 1917, the battle of Pilken Ridge[12] had pushed the German line back and Artillery Wood, east of the Yser canal. This was then captured by the Guards Division. When the fighting in this area was over the cemetery was constructed and remained as a front line cemetery until 1918.

John was killed in action on the 4th August 1917 and is buried in the cemetery named Artillery Wood near the village of Boezinge. This area was facing the German front line over the Yser canal.

John's death was reported in the Totnes and Mid Devon News[13] on the 18th August 1917, the article read:

'Much deep sympathy is felt with Mr and Mrs Salter and family at the death of their eldest son. John Ernest, who was killed in action in France

on the 4th inst. Deceased was a well-liked, good tempered, promising young man, working with his father as an outfitter until a year ago when he joined the colours when he reached the age limit. He progressed rapidly as a soldier, and was soon in the fighting line, but now has fallen doing his duty to King and Country at the early age of 20 years. On Sunday special reference was made to the death in the parish Church and the 'Dead March' was played at the close of each service'.

Pte. 196573 John Ernest Salter aged, aged 20 was killed in action or died of wounds on the 4th August 1917, it is not known which. He was awarded the British War Medal and the Victory Medal and is remembered in St Petroc's Church, South Brent as well as St Mary's Church, Warwick where his name is inscribed on the Warwickshire Regimental Memorial.

The South Brent Parish Magazine[14] carried an article on John under the heading of 'The Roll of Honour':

Parishioners were much grieved to hear that Mr. and Mrs. Salter had received the sad news of the death of their beloved son, Ernest, whilst fighting at the front. One is glad to hear that in subsequent letters from the Captain of the regiment, they were informed that his death was instantaneous and therefore painless.

Many of the older residents of South Brent will remember Salter's shop in Station Road run by George Salter, the younger brother of John Ernest Salter. George Salter had a daughter and two sons, one son was also a John. He was the nephew of John Ernest. John was well known in the village and was a member of the Church Choir. He died in 2004. The shop once owned by the Salter's became a flower shop, an electronics shop and now it is a hair stylist.

NOTES

1 John Hambling Salter was born in Avonwick; his birth was registered in the 1st quarter of 1867, Totnes District Vol. 5b. Page, 206. He died on the 23rd June 1940. Probate was granted to his widow, Mary and sons George and Horace. The amount was £4048 2/4d.

2 Mary Elizabeth Reeves was born in Stokenham, Kingsbridge, Devon about 1872.

3 London Metropolitan Parish Records.

4 John Ernest Salter was born in the 4th quarter of 1896 his birth was registered in the Fulham District of London, Vol. 1a. Page,235.

5 Kelly's Directory 1910, Page 104.

6 George Edward Salter was born in the 3rd quarter of 1901. His birth was registered in the Fulham District, Vol.1a. Page, 214.

7 Vera Rosina Salter was born in the 2nd quarter of 1904. Her birth was registered in the Totnes District, Vol. 5a. Page, 158.

8 Horace Salter was born on the 12th February 1906, his birth was registered in the Totnes District, Vol. 5a.Page 158.It appears that Horace married a Miss Holman in Plympton in the 4th quarter of 1929 and he died in April 1998, aged 92.

9 Agnes Joyce Salter was born in the 1st quarter of 1908 and registered in the Totnes District, Vol. 5a. Page 157. She married William Henry Arthur Maynard (1907-1993) in the 3rd quarter of 1931, registered in the Totnes District, Vol.5a. Page, 443. It appears that Agnes died in February1932, there is one child, William Henry Denis Maynard, whose birth date is February 1932

10 Courtesy of Mrs M. Eales Archive.

[11] *Atkinson, C.T. Devon's Regimental History.*

[12] The battle of Pilken Ridge was one of the phases of the 3rd Battle of Ypres, 31st Juyl-2nd August 1917.

[13] *Courtesy of the Totnes and Mid Devon News.*

[14] This piece from the Parish Magazine by courtesy of Mrs M. Eales Archive.

Leonard Howard Shillabeer
1897 – 1918

Leonard was born in South Brent in 1897 to Thomas and Ethel Shillabeer. He had two older and one younger sisters. Ruby, (1892) Elizabeth, (1894) and Ivy (1899). His father's occupation was a Plate Layer for the Great Western Rail Company, his mother was a housewife.

They all lived at 34 Church Street, South Brent. It is worth noting that at number 35 Church Street resided William and Mary Shillabeer (grandparents to Leonard) with their grandson Alfred (13). According to the census these were Thomas's father and mother.

(*At number 36 Church Street lived Bertie Charles Hard, M M who is also included in this work and died in 1917)*

The 1911 census shows Leonard was an errand boy of 14, still living at home, 34 Church Street.

According to Leonard's medal records, he enlisted on the 19th January 1915, but on the *'Roll of Individuals Entitled to the War Badge'* records he is shown as enlisting on the 5th September 1914.[1] Both documents do confirm his regiment as '*The Devonshire Regiment*', and the Parish War Memorial has Leonard being a member of the 2nd Battalion of the Devonshire Regiment.

There is no record of him in Atkinson's work, '*The Devonshire Regiment*'. His army number is 10928 indicating he joined Kitchener's first army.

Looking at his date(s) of entry into the Army, his training would have taken about three months before he would have been shipped out to France. Working on these time line, Leonard would probably have joined the Forth Army, 23rd Infantry Brigade, 8th division, under General Sir Henry Rawlinson. This cannot be verified because of the conflicting entry dates.

There is every possibility that he was at the Battle of Auber's (9th May 1915) this was a pincer movement attack on the Germans at Auber's Ridge, just north of Arras, France. The *Northern* pincer would be made by 8th Division, moving south-east towards Rouges Bancs, and then spreading to capture the line between Fromelles and La Cliqueterie. This was the plan but it did not work due to the strong German defences.

This offensive was a disaster for the British and the 8th Division (2nd Devon's) in that one day there were 4682 casualties of whom 192 were officers. More than 11,000 British casualties were sustained on 9 May 1915, the vast majority within yards of their own front-line trench. Mile for mile, Division for Division, this was one of the highest rates of loss during the entire war.

It appears that Leonard survived this battle and the action at Boius Grenier. This was also a diversary action to confuse the Germans prior to the main Somme offensive. He was in all probability involved in the action of the Battle of Albert, 1st – 13th July 1916, the first phase of the Battle of the Somme.

It must be assumed that Leonard was wounded here as he was discharged from the army on the 26th July 1917 to pension due to disability. His medal record states that he was awarded the British War Medal, the Victory Medal and the 1915 Star. As stated earlier he was also awarded the War Badge on his discharge from the army.[2]

Leonard died from a '*cold*' 4th January 1918. The following article appeared in the Totnes and Mid Devon News on the 12th January 1918:

'*The death of Lance Cpl. L. H. Shillabeer of South Brent, took place on Friday. He volunteered at the outbreak of war and served with the Devon's in many engagements, being severely wounded and losing his left eye and left leg. He was discharged from the army on pension and his death followed a violent cold. On Wednesday a good number of people were at the graveside as well as in the Church. Six soldiers bore the deceased to the grave. The organist played the death march.*

Leonard's Headstone
Photo: Author

Leonard is buried in the Churchyard of St Petroc's Church at South Brent. It is not known why he does not have a Commonwealth War Grave headstone as was the custom then for soldiers that had died as a result of injuries. His grave stone was privately funded by the family and has been damaged probably by branches from the yew tree very close to his grave.[3]

NOTES

1 National Archive record of War Badge Awards.

2 Badge Number and Certificate 253022, age 22 years, issued 26/7/1917. Reason for discharge, Wounded.

3 It is hoped that Leonard's headstone will be repaired by the parish before the 2018 centenary.

George Smallridge
1882 – 1917

George Smallridge[1] was the eldest son of George[2] and Annie (nee Putt[3]) Smallridge, who lived at 4 Stidston, South Brent. According to the 1891 census, George had four younger brothers and sisters, William[4] 7, John Henry[5] 5, Elizabeth Ann[6] 3, and Emily Jane[7]. George senior was employed as an Agriculture Labourer.

The 1901 census shows the family had grown by another four children, Blanch[8] 8, Fredrick[9] 6, Lily 3 and Charles Reginald[10] and were living at 21 Church Street, South Brent.

On the 1911 the family was living at Wellington Square, Church Street, another child had been born between the census, Daisy[11], 8. It also shows that Annie had 10 children all living.

As for George Smallridge, he is not on the 1901 census for some reason. He had married Sarah Statt[12] in 1903 and set up home in Station Road, South Brent. They had two children, Emmeline May[13] 7 and Alfred George 6.[14] Both of which are recorded on the 1911 census. George was employed in the mill at Brent as a Flock Maker.

It is thought George enlisted in Totnes in or around 1914[15], his number, 26327 suggests he was part of Kitchener's second army (K2 the second one hundred thousand volunteers) raised in Exeter in 1914 and attached to the Divisional Troops of the 20th (Light)

Division. If this was the case he would have commenced training and completing it before July 1915, when the Battalion was prepared to leave for France on the 28th July 1915 arriving at Le Havre. The 9th Battalion then became part of the 20th Brigade of the 7th Division.

As there are no records to refer to it is not known for certain what actions George took part in, what is known about the 9th Battalion is that they took part in the Battle of Bullcourt between the 7th and 10th May 1917. There were fewer casualties in this conflict compared to others with only 23 killed, 7 missing and 94 wounded.

As George died from his wounds some five weeks after this battle it seems a long time he was in a casualty clearing station, therefore it is unlikely he was injured in this battle.

The 9th Battalion were not in an active action again until the middle of June. The German trenches were some distance away but they continued to send in shell fire, sniper attacks and machine gun bursts, this did little to interfere with the day to day life of the British. During this period there were causalities and it could have been possible that during one of these skirmish attacks that George was wounded.

The village where George is buried is Achiet-Le-Grand[16], between April 1917 and March 1918, the village was occupied by the 45th and 49th Causality Clearing Stations[17]. It could be safe to assume that George was wounded sometime during this period and was taken to this casualty area where he died and is buried. This theory is backed up by C.T. Atkinson's work on the Devon Regiment. In total there are 13 men from the Devonshire Regiment buried in this cemetery.

News of the death of George Smallridge was published in the Totnes and Mid Devon News on the 7th July 1917. The article read:

'News was received at South Brent on Saturday morning that Pte. George Smallridge of the Devon's was killed in action in France on June 23rd. The deceased leaves a widow and two children'[18].

His brother, Fredrick[19] also served during the war in the Machine gun Corp and returned home when hostilities ended.

George Smallridge, aged 35, Private 26327, 9th Battalion Devonshire Regiment rests in grave 1M, 12, he left a widow, Sarah and two children, Emmeline and Alfred in South Brent. He was awarded the British War Medal and the Victory Medal.

NOTES

1 George Smallridge was born in the 1st quarter of 1882; his birth was registered in the Totnes District, Vol. 5b.Page42.

2 Born 1858, married in Totnes 1881,

3 Annie was born about 1860

4 William was born in the 1st quarter of 1883, Totnes District, Vol. 5b, Page 209

5 John Henry was born in the 1st quarter of 1886, Totnes District Vol. 5b, Page 197.

[6] Elizabeth Ann was born in the 2nd quarter of 1888, Totnes District, Vol. 5b, Page 187

[7] Emily Jane was born in the 2nd quarter of 1890, Totnes District, Vol. 5b, Page 177

[8] Born about 1893 at South Brent

[9] Born about 1895,

[10] Born in the 1st quarter of 1900, Totnes District, Vol. 5b. Page, 156

[11] Born about 1903 at South Brent.

[12] Sarah was born about 1881, married George in the 3rd quarter of 1902, Totnes District Vol. 5b, Page 338.

[13] Emmeline May was born in the 3rd quarter of 1903, Totnes District Vol. 5b, Page 151. Married James Hannaford in 1st quarter of 1925, Totnes District, Vol. 5b, Page 303, died December 1961, Exeter District, Vol. 7a, Page 415

[14] Alfred George was born in South Brent, in the 2nd quarter of 1905, Totnes District, Vol. 5b Page153.

[15] George's Army records do not now exist as they were amongst the many destroyed in WW2 by a German raid on the repository, destroying many thousands of the records.

[16] Achiet-Le-Grand is a village 19 kilometres South of Arras, France.

[17] Achiet-le-Grand was occupied by the 7th Bedford's on 17 March 1917, lost on 25 March 1918 after a defence by the 1st/6th Manchester's, and recaptured on 23 August 1918. From April 1917 to March 1918, the village was occupied by the 45th and 49th Casualty Clearing Stations. Achiet station was an allied railhead.

[18] *Courtesy Totnes and Mid Devon News, 7th July 1917.*

[19] See 'Men from South Brent who are known to have enlisted for service'.

Daniel Thomas Squires
1881 – 1916

Thomas Daniel Squires was born in South Brent in 1881[1] to Daniel and Elizabeth (nee Furze) Squires; he was the fifth of eight children[2]. His name was officially registered at as Thomas Daniel but somewhere his name has been transposed to Daniel Thomas.

Daniel Thomas and his brother Archibald are still at school when the 1891 census was taken, aged 9 and 7. The family was living in Aish Village.

The 1891 census described Daniel (senior) as a gardener and his daughter, Elizer Ann (18) as a domestic, Daniel, junior, was not the first to join the Royal Navy. His elder brother Alfred[3] had joined the Navy as a career choice prior to 1901[4].

On the 1901 census for *'Vessels'* Alfred is shown as a Stoker, aged 24 on HMS Ocean[5]. It is thought that Daniel joined the Royal Navy not to long after the census date.

Daniel Thomas married Selina Alice Yabsley (1884-1971[6]) in the 1st quarter of 1907 at Kingsbridge, Devon.[7] On the 1911 census she was the head of the house and residing in Loddiswell with their one year old son, Thomas Henry.[8] Daniel was not shown on this census, it is fair to assume that he was at sea. Also residing with Selena was her brother, Robert Henry Yabsley[9].

On the 30th June 1914 Daniel was awarded a Good Conduct Medal on board HMS Indefatigable[10] by the Commander in Chief of the Mediterranean fleet. Danial held the rank of a Petty Officer Stoker.

At the beginning of the First War, HMS Indefatigable was part of the 2nd Battle Cruiser Squadron (BCS) in the Mediterranean. After a refit in Malta she returned to the UK in February 1915 and re-joined the 2nd BCS and became part of Vice Admiral Sir David Beatty's Battle Cruiser Fleet.

From February 1915, and for the next eighteen months, she conducted uneventful patrols of the North Sea, and became the temporary Flagship of the 2nd Battle Cruiser Squadron during April–May 1916.

When the German fleet were preparing to came out from their harbour's into the Skagerrak, [North Sea] *Room 22*[11] at the Admiralty knew when they [the German Fleet] were actually sailing out and sent this vital information to Admiral Beatty and the Grand Fleet based at Scapa Flow in Scotland. The Grand Fleet put to sea immediately, before the German fleet had left port.

When the German Fleet were off the Danish coast near Jutland, Admiral Franz Von Hipper's Battle Cruisers spotted Beatty's Battle Cruiser Fleet to their west at 3:20 p.m. on the 31st May, Beatty's ships did not spot the Germans to their east until 3:30pm, a full ten minutes later. Beatty's Battle Cruisers opened fire at 3:48pm on the 31st May 1916; the Battle of Jutland had started.

HMS Indefatigable was hit at 1605hours, 17 minutes into the action[12]. She was hit several times in the first few minutes of the "*Run to the South*", the opening phase of the Battle Cruiser action. Shells from the German Battle Cruiser *Von der Tann* hit Indefatigable causing an explosion which ripped a hole in her hull, a second explosion hurled large pieces of the ship 200 feet (60 m) in the air.

After the last explosion, only two of the crew of 1,019 surviving. Amongst the men who died was Petty Officer Stoker Daniel Thomas Squires, from South Brent.

Daniel is still on board HMS Indefatigable and will be there for eternity. His name along with others who died that day is inscribed on the Plymouth Naval Memorial, the Loddiswell War memorial and also the South Brent Memorial. He left a wife and a son aged 7.

Plymouth Naval Memorial[13]
Courtesy of the Commonwealth War Graves Commission.

Loddiswell Village War Memorial
Photo: Author's collection

NOTES

[1] Birth registered at Totnes in the 2nd quarter of 1881, Vol. 5b, Page 200.

[2] Children of Daniel and Elizabeth Squires, Susan, b.1871, Eliza, B. 1873, Alfred, b. 1876, Fred, b.1878, Daniel, b. 1882, Archibald, b.1884, Winifred, b.1887 and Ethel, b. 1908.

[3] Arthur was Born in 1876 Barnstable, Vol. 5b, Page 441

[4] Alfred is shown as a servant in Barnstable in 1891, aged 15

[5] HMS Ocean was commissioned at Devonport on 20 February 1900 and served in the Mediterranean Fleet until January 1901, when she was transferred to the China Station in response to the Boxer Rebellion. In September 1902, she suffered damage in a typhoon, and then underwent a refit that lasted into 1903.

[6] Selina was born, 11th May 1884, died September 1971 age 87, death registered at Kingsbridge, Vol.7a. Page 1203

[7] Marriage registered in the 1st quarter of 1907, Kingsbridge District, Vol. 5b, Page 349.

[8] Born 26th December 1909, Kingsbridge, Married 1930 to Constance Hingston, he died November 1996, aged 86.

[9] Joined the 13th Devon's, Works Battalion, in September 1916 at Exeter, Number 40371.Discharged unfit April 1917.

[10] HMS Indefatigable was a Battle cruiser of the Royal Navy and the lead ship of her class.

[11] Room 22 was the secret encrypting room in the Admiralty which was able to intercept German radio information.

[12] HMS Queen Mary was hit and destroyed at 1622, 18 minutes later. The Rev George Stanley Kewney, from South Brent was lost in this sinking.

[13] Courtesy of the Commonwealth War Graves Commission.

Arthur Roland Taylor
1896 – 1918

Arthur Roland Taylor was not born in South Brent; he originates from Ilford, Essex and was born in 1896[1] to Robert Cyril Taylor[2] and Edith Mary Taylor, nee Newbald[3]. He had an elder brother Robert Collingwood[4] and three younger brother's Thomas[5], Vincent Corbett[6], and Charles Stewart[7].

On the 1901 census Arthur was aged five and lived with his parents at Connan Quay, Flintshire. His father was an estate agent there and the household had four domestic staff, a house keeper, under maid, cook and nurse. By the time of the 1911 census the family had moved to Beagle Late House, Bridlington, Yorkshire, there were now a further two siblings, Vincent and Charles, and their father was now working as a Land Agent.

Arthur left England for Canada in April 1913, sailing on the Tunisian, arriving at Quebec on the 27th April; he was aged 17 at the time. It is not known when exactly when he joined the Canadian Flying Corps but it is thought to be in or around June 1917, where he gained his flying wings.

In or about November 1917 he returned to England to join the Royal Flying Corps, (RFC) and was promoted to the rank of 2nd Lieutenant and sent to either East Boldre[8] or Beaulieu airfields in Hampshire to complete his training, both are very close to each other.

It was on the 19th January 1918 that Arthur was involved in a flying accident where he was killed. The official report on the accident gives the reason for the fatality as '*Pilot Error*'[9]. He is buried in the Church yard of St Paul's, East Boldre alongside other airmen who died whilst on active service.

The news of Arthurs's death was published in the Totnes and Mid Devon News on 26th January 1918.

The Article read:

SOUTH BRENT AIRMAN KILLED

'*Mr and Mrs Taylor of Millswood House, South Brent have received news that their eldest son, Second-Lieut. A.R. Taylor, RFC; was killed on Saturday by an accident to his machine whilst flying at Beaulieu. Lieut. Taylor, aged 21 was formally in Canada as a flying instructor.*'

Arthur was educated at Berkhamsted School in Hertfordshire and his name is on the school chapel war memorial. It reads only: ***'Taylor, A. R.'***

Arthur was awarded the Victory Medal and The British War Medal. Information on his medal card states that the medals were sent to his mother, who had left South Brent and resided in Birkenhead.

The Flight and Aircraft Engineer Magazine of 31st January 1918 records the death of Arthur, the eulogy is similar to that of the Totnes paper article, with the following additional information:

'He was educated at Berkhamsted School and went to America in March 1913. He joined the Canadian RFC in June 1917, gained his wings and came to England to finish his training in last November'.[10]

Headstone in St Pauls Church yard
East Boldre, Hampshire
Photo: Author

NOTES

[1] Arthur Roland was born in the 2nd quarter of 1896, birth registered in the Romford District of Essex, Vol. 4a. Page 437.

[2] Robert Cyril Taylor; born Rothbury, Northumberland 1860. Married Edith Mary Newbald, 1st quarter 1892, Beverly, Yorkshire.

[3] Ethel Mary Newbald, born 4th quarter 1861in the Hull District, Yorkshire.

[4] Robert was born 3rd quarter 1893, West Ham Essex. Vol. 4a. Page 155. He left from Liverpool in March 1913 for New York arriving on the 13th March. It appears that he was the Assistant Purser on the Caronia as he is on the ship's crew list from Sierra Leone to New York. He married Katie Ruth Johnson (1897-1979) in

Barnaby, British Columbia, and died in Vancouver Canada in January 1978, ager 84.

5 Thomas was born about 1900 in Flintshire, married Mona Alice Houston (1898) from Hendon in Woollahra South Australia in 1926 and died in April 1976 at Armadale, NSW.

6 Vincent was born in the 4th quarter of 1900 in Flintshire. He left for Canada in 1919, aged 18. Occupation, RAF. He left England again for Canada in 1930, occupation, Insurance Business; he died in British Columbia in 1968.

7 Charles was born about 1904.

8 An airfield was built in East Boldre in 1910. There was a flying school here for two years before the airfield reverted to quiet grazing land, but in 1914 one of the sheds on the airfield was taken over by the Royal Flying Corps and by 1915 the demand for pilots for World War I was so great that a training school, called RFC Beaulieu was built on the area. The camp was closed in 1919.

9 Source, RAF Museum Archives, London.

10 *Flight and Aircraft Engineer, 31st January 1918, page 134.*

Wallace Tozer
1893-1916

Wallace was born in the 2nd quarter of 1893 to John and Lucinda (Lucy) Tozer[1], (nee Muridge or Moridge, from North Huish, 1861-1908) residing at Rattery, Devon. He was the youngest of three boys; his brothers were Alfred 12[2], and William Henry 10. (1891 3rd qtr.) On the 1901 census he is aged seven.

The 1911 census shows that Wallace's mother, Lucy was missing, she had died in 1908; John (father) is shown as a widower. The household now shows a daughter, Emily; aged 27 living with them she is described as 'Housekeeper'[3]. Alfred and William are shown as farm labourers and Wallace is a groom/domestic.

There is no record to show that Alfred was called up or served in the forces during the Great War.

William, his older brother, immigrated to Canada (Quebec) on the SS Ascania, a steam liner of the Cunard Line from Southampton on the 11th June 1912. His occupation is shown as a labourer. He enlisted with the Canadian Expeditionary Forces and was in the 146th Battalion[4], his number was 835176.

On his entry form, which he signed on the 27th December 1915, he gives his place of birth as Rattery and Emily his sister as his next of kin. She is now residing at Island House, South Brent. William survived the war and returned to Canada, where he remained until his death. He died on the 7th August 1936 in Frontenac, Canada of Tuberculosis and kidney failure age 46.

Wallace Tozer married Dorothy Oxenholm in 1914[5] their first and only child was born in December 1914 at South Brent. He was named Wallace John Tozer.

As far as it can be determined, Wallace enlisted at Newton Abbot into the 9th (Service) Battalion of the Devonshire Regiment, formed in Exeter in September 1914. When he enlisted is not known but going by his army number (20642) he could well have been late 1914 or early 1915 when Kitchener called for his new army (K2)[6].

It is very probable that Wallace took part in the battle of Loos (25th September 1915 until 19th October 1915). The 7th Division, of which the 9th Devon's were part of, 5,224 officer's men and in this battle, The 8th Devon's lost 619 officers and men in the attack on Hullich.

The next action the 20th Light Division took part in was the Battle of Mount Sorrel. (2nd June-13th June 1916) The action described took place between Hill 60 at Zwarteleen and Hooge. Much of this area was wooded.

The next military action occurred on 1st July 1916, this battle was to go down in history as the day Britain sustained 60,000 casualties, of which 20,000 men were killed in the first hour of battle. Of those

20,000 killed Wallace Tozer was one of these casualties. This was the first day of the **Battle of the Somme.**

British artillery had been shelling the German held lines for several days prior to the attack on the 1st but the Germans were dug in deep, and the shelling had little effect. The 9th Service Battalion of the Devon's were positioned at Mansel Copse and ordered to attack a 400 yard wide sector of the front line opposite Mametz; this was part of the 20th brigade's attack.[7] Meanwhile the 8th Devon's were held back in the reserve lines.

The 9th were positioned between the 2nd Borders, (on their left) and the 2nd Gordon Highlanders, (on their right.) The 9th attacked in two waves, Number '1' and '2' companies were in the first wave with the 4th and 3rd companies attacking in the second wave.

The Germans were well positioned and protected by machine guns positioned in the Shrine, firing 450 rounds a minute at a range of 800 yards. The effect of this was to inflict very heavy causalities on the first wave of the 9th. Out of the 775 men in the 9th service battalion, 149 officers and ranks were killed, 277 wounded and 55 missing in action, a total of 480 men. The 1st and 3rd companies suffered the most casualties.

Later 123 bodies of men from the 9th Devon's and 38 bodies of the 8th Devon's were recovered from the battle field and were buried on the 4th July 1916. The service of burial was carried out by the

Reverend E.C. Crosse, the 9th. Battalion Chaplin. These men, including Wallace Tozer, were buried in a mass grave on the former British front line trench at Mansel Copse. The copse overlooks the site of the battle. A temporary wooden cross marked the place where eighteen Devon men were buried.

The burial trench first used has now become the Devonshire Cemetery, Mametz.[8]

Private Wallace Tozer' headstone
Photo by Conrad Heath

Private Wallace Tozer was killed on the first day of the Battle of the Somme. The Totnes and Mid Devon News reported his death on the 29th July 1916.

The article read:

News has been received that Pte. Wallace Tozer of South Brent was killed in action in France. The bells of the parish Church were slowly chimed on Sunday and the 'Dead March' was played as tribute to his memory.[9]

On the 5th August 1916 there was a small article on the memorial service at Rattery Church, It read;

Memorial service was held for three brave lads.Pvt. Reginald Horseman, Pvt Archie Joint and Pvt Wallace Tozer all from the 9th Devon's. The Rev. C.C Broimaldie officiated and preached a supportive sermon. This little village can claim a record, of a population of 250, 42 men are serving, 5 killed, 4 wounded and one POW. [10]

Rattery War Memorial at the entrance to the Church
Photo: Author

Private Wallace Tozer was posthumously awarded the Victory and British War medals. His name was placed on the Rattery War Memorial at the entrance to the Church. He left a wife and young son.

There is a memorial stone to the Devon Regiment which has the following inscription:

The Devonshire's held this trench
The Devonshire Regiment hold it still

Memorial stone to the Devon Regiment
Photo: Author's collection

NOTES

[1] Lucy or Louisa died 2nd quarter 1908, Totnes District, Vol. 5b Page 133

[2] Alfred Tozer (1889- 1963) married Ellen Finning, Newton Abbot, 2nd quarter 1913, Vol. 5b, Page 254. Ellen died in 1942 at Newton Abbot.

[3] It is interesting to note that the census of 1911 asks how many children the parents have had. In this case there were seven born of which six are surviving? Lucy was eleven years younger than her husband John. The other children were Emily, John and Thomas. The mother of these children is not confirmed as Louisa.

[4] The 146th Battalion was formed in late 1915. It left Canada in September 1916 and became part of the 95th Battalion C.E.F.

[5] Totnes district, vol. 5b, page 399.

[6] The 9th (Service) Battalion was formed at Exeter on 15 September 1914 as part of Lord Kitchener's new army, (K2) they were attached as Divisional Troops to the 20th (Light) Division. In April 1915: they left the Division and landed at Le Havre 28 July 1915. On 8 August 1915: they came under orders of 20th Brigade, 7th Division along with the 8th Battalion of the Devonshire Regiment.

[7] Mametz is a village on the Somme which is 6.5 kilometres east of Albert. It was within the German lines on the 1st July 1916, and was captured by the 7th Division. Mametz wood was finally cleared of the German army by the 7th July.

[8] The Photos were taken in March 2012 and are from the author's collection.

[9] Courtesy of *'The Totnes and Mid Devon News', 29th July 1916.*

[10] Ibid 5th August 1916.

James White
1889 – 1918

James was born in North Huish in the 3rd quarter of 1889[1] and was the fourth child of John[2] and Martha nee Brambury[3] White. The other children in the family were Jeffrey 11[4], John 8[5] and Annie 5.

James White
From the Sandry Archive

The family resided at Number 1, Old Plymouth Road, North Huish, Avonwick, Devon. James father was a bootmaker by profession and is shown on the 1891 census as an employer of staff. It appears from the census that he was employing William Crocker 27, who also lodged with the family. All the children with the exception of James were at school.

By the time the 1901 census was taken, the family had moved from North Huish to South Brent, more precisely, The London Inn. John

White, senior, is shown as the Licensed Victualler and Bootmaker employing staff. The staff listed were his sons, Jeffrey 21, and John 18 and Annie 15[6]. Annie is described as a *'worker at home'*. What is not known is whether she was employed as a barmaid or boot maker. James, who was only 11, was still at school.

The 1911 census does not show Annie, she had married[7] Richard Hind[8] at least four years earlier, as on the census return there is a girl called Alice Martha Hind, aged 3 a grand-daughter. Looking at Annie's census return it appears that her daughter Alice was staying with her grand-parents as she [Annie] had just had another child.[9]

John senior is shown on this census. Again, as a Hotel Proprietor and Boot Maker. The three boys, Jeffery 31, John 28 and James 21 are all listed as *'Assistants in the Business'.*

From a note on the Army medal record of James, he enlisted at Torquay, into the 1st Battalion of the Devonshire Regiment. At some point he joined or was seconded to the Royal Warwickshire regiment. This is confirmed as in the photo James, illustrated earlier, is wearing the Warwickshire regiment cap badge.

In April 1916, whilst home in South Brent on leave he appeared as a witness at the inquest of his brother, John. *(Appendix 1)* The newspaper at the time reported that he was in the 3rd Hussars, a Cavalry Regiment.

Very little information has been found out about James army service. All his records were destroyed during the second war leaving a small amount of information in the National Archives. James was issued with the army number 31156, whilst with the 1st Devon's and the 10th Royal Warwickshire Regiment, then army number 28031 when he was with the 8th Hussars. There are no dates shown as to when James joined the 1st Devon's in Torquay.[10] He is also listed in the Roll of Individuals entitled to the Victory Medal.

James sent silk Easter greetings cards from the front to his mother and niece, Alice Hind, both residing at the London Inn, South Brent. There are no postmarks on the cards so it is impossible to say what Easter they relate to.

James died on the 23rd June 1918 in France from wounds received in battle. News of the death was published in the Totnes and Mid Devon News on 30th July 1918, the article read:

'Much sympathy is express for Mrs White, of the London Inn, South Brent, who have received news that their youngest son, Jas White (Hussars) died on June 23rd of wounds received in action'. [11]

The same article reported on the death of Richard Hard, Stoker who had recently joined the Royal Navy.

James was buried at the Thiennes British Cemetery on the outskirts of the village[12]. He is buried in Row C, grave number 12. The cemetery was started by the 5th Division in May 1918 and continued in use until August 1918, when it was then used by the 59th and 61st Divisions.

He is also remembered on the family grave in St Petroc's grave yard South Brent, where on the large headstone at the White family plot there is an inscription and memorial to James White.

In accordance to the King's wishes, the White family were awarded the bronze grave plaque with his name inscribed upon it.[13]

Bronze grave plaque

James was also remembered on a wall mounted memorial along with four other South Brent men who were members of the Odd Fellows Lodge, in South Brent[14]. Lodge Alexandria 5236 met in the Pack Horse pub in South Brent . This memorial was unveiled in April 1920 and the event was reported on in the Totnes and Mid Devon News. The memorial itself has not been seen for many years and the hunt is on to try and find it. James White was awarded the British War Medal and the Victory medal.

Further information on the White family.

John White, senior, died in March 1916, the funeral arrangements were carried out by A.W. Cranch[15]. This ledger page from the Cranch archive shows the cost and arrangements for the funeral for John senior in March 1916, the next entry shows the name and funeral details for John Junior three days later. (See Appendix 2) These ledgers also have the arrangements that were made and costs for Martha White, who died in 1941 and her son Jeffrey who died in 1943

James White was the Great Uncle of Mike Sandry, Motor mechanic and engineer in the village up until his retirement some years ago. His mother was Alice Sandry (Nee, Hind,) James's niece from his older sister Annie Hind.[16]

Postscript

Mrs Jean Sandry, with her daughters and grandchildren visited the grave of James White in November 2014. They all found it a very moving experience. Their trip also included Tyne-Cott cemetery and Hill 62.

Appendix 1

Totnes and Mid Devon News, April 1st. 1916

Headline,

Inquest.

Sub Heading,

South Brent Tragedy.

Worried about having to join the army.

Mr Hacker, (coroner) held an inquest on Friday into the cause of the death of John White, at South Brent.

Inspector Poultrey, representative of the Great Western Railway, and Superintendent Jeffery, the Police. Mr A.W. Cranch, Foreman of the Jury. Many members of the family and public were also present.

Private James White, 3rd Hussars, stated that he had not seen the body of his brother but had seen the clothes, all of which he identified.

Superintendent Jeffery stated it was impossible for anyone to identify the body owing to the mutilation. Witness stated he was satisfied that they were the remains of John White, aged 32. He could give no reason for death.

Witness (James White) came home on March 21, owing to the death of his father. His brother had fits several times recently. Deceased lived at home with parents and was a shoe maker. Saw him

Wednesday morning when he brought him a cup of tea in bedroom. There was nothing in his manner to lead the witness to think he had any intention of taking his own life.

Mrs Barbara Hard, Widow, stated that deceased, on Wednesday morning brought her a cup of tea, as she slept in the house that night. He did not take breakfast, but brought in milk then went out, nothing out of the ordinary.

She had seen him fit; he had several in the last fortnight. She knew he was disturbed about his father's death. The coroner observed that the mother was unfit to give evidence, and witness said that she did not know anything sufficient to cause extra worry.

Deceased went to Ivybridge on Monday, returned Tuesday morning about 6 am. Appears to have lost his memory, went to bed, but talked of going to Newton Abbot to join the army. He received call up papers on March 30th. On Tuesday morning he did not know what he was talking about.

James Addiscott, Engine driver, started he left Exeter at 0830, train to Plymouth, coming toward Brent, just passing mail apparatus on the down road, about half mile from Brent station, saw a man approaching along the footpath, the postman or poachers path. Deceased walked up some distance on the up line and walked along with his hands in his pockets, between the rails. He blew the whistle as always on approach to Brent.

Deceased stopped about 200 yards away, watched the train and suddenly dashed from the up line right in front of the engine. Witness applied the brakes, pulling the train up. The body was found under the third coach. The train moved on to Brent station and the incident was reported to the station master.

Inspector Poultry stated that the foot path was a track used by postal workers and not for public access. The deceased was trespassing.

John Taylor, chauffeur of South Brent stated deceased was known to have fits.

Dr Slater, deceased was decapitated and one arm torn off. He knew he had fits but had not seen them He said it was signs of epilepsy.

Recorded Verdict: That he threw himself under a train due to temporary insanity.

NOTES

1 Ref. Totnes District, Vol. 5b. Page 179.

2 John White died on the 19th March 1916 after a riding Accident. He is buried in the family tomb at South Brent.

3 Martha was born in about 1884 and died in November 1941.

4 Jeffrey White died in 1943, aged 63. Buried in the family tomb at South Brent.

5 John White died 22nd March 1916, 3 days after his father. See the coroner's report Appendix 2

[6] Annie Hind, nee White died September 1973, aged 87, Registered in the Plymouth District, Vol.7a Page 1752

[7] Annie Agnes White married Richard Reginald Hind, in about 1908. He originated from Ugborough.

[8] Richard Hind died June 1969, aged 81, Registered at Plymouth District, Vol. 7a, Page 1491.

[9] On the 1911 census, Richard and Annie had two other children, Mable 2 and Richard, one month. It appears that John and Martha were babysitting the eldest child, Alice. Richard Hind was a farmer at Lower Chelston, South Brent.

[10] National Archive Record, WO329/811.

[11] Totnes and Mid Devon News, 30th July 1918.

[12] Private James White is buried in Row C Grave 12 of the cemetery.

[13] The plaque is still in the families care.

[14] Lodge Alexandria was founded in 1864 and met in the Pack Horse Public House. It is not known when it stopped working. The Odd Fellows were nearly all journey men, skilled craftsmen who had not been indentured.

[15] Courtesy of Mrs Rene Cranch and the Cranch Archive.

[16] Grateful thanks to the family for the Information and Photographs of James, and the Death Penny

Walter Thomas Mortimore
1877 – 1915

Walter was born in Ugborough in the first quarter of 1877, and his birth was registered in the Totnes District register, (Vol.5b. page 209). Walter is shown in the 1881 census as child aged four years old. He is living with his family in Bigbury Village, where his father was an agriculture labourer. The family consisted of an elder brother, Albert Samuel, (5)[1] Walter Thomas (4) Arthur H, (2) and Fredrick, (1 month)[2].

The 1891 census shows William and Ellen (as Elizabeth), nee Goodman, now living at Averton Gifford with children, Fredrick, (10) Alice (6)[3] and Emma (1)[4].

There is an interesting additional entry on the return, John Goodman, (19), described on the census as "*Wife's Child*". There is no record of Walter who would be fourteen or fifteen by now. It would be common for a boy of that age to be working elsewhere and not shown on the family return.

Walter's naval record show that he was born in 'North Brent' and joined the Royal Navy on the 24th January 1896, signing on for 12 years. He is recorded as being a labourer prior to joining up.

In the second quarter of 1899, Walter married Emma Jane Skinner in Devonport. It is not known where they lived after they married.

Walter's service record shows him on board the ship, HMS Vivid at the time as a stoker in 1901.

1911 is when Walter appears in the census return; he is serving on board H.M.S. Tamar, stationed in China and is shown as married, aged thirty four. This is confirmed by the return submitted by his wife, Emma Mortimore. Her return states that she was born in Kingsbridge, and is aged thirty two years old, living in Loddiswell as the head of the house. She has a daughter aged ten and her aged mother living with her. Walter's brother, Albert is at Calstock in Cornwall.

By 1911, Walter's parents and family had again moved back to Harbourneford, South Brent where his father William is a farm labourer. He still has John (Goodman) Mortimore, (39) living with them on the farm. John is now married with two children, William and Ernest[6], but there is no mention on the census of his wife. Walter's younger siblings, Ellen (15) is a domestic, Bertie (17) a general labourer and Beatrice (13) still at school.

Walter was still a serving naval rating when the First World War commenced in August 1914. He was on board H.M.S. Goliath, a Canopus Class pre-dreadnought battleship.

Goliath was assigned to the 8th Battle Squadron, operating out of Devonport. HMS Goliath was then transferred to the East Indies Station on 20 September to support cruisers on convoy duty in the

Middle East, escorting an Indian convoy to the Persian Gulf and German East Africa until October.

HMS Golieth then took part in the blockade of the German light cruiser SMS Königsberg in the Rufiji River, (German Eat Africa until November, 1914 during which crew member Commander Henry Peel Ritchie won the Victoria Cross. Golieth bombarded Dar-es-Salaam on 28 November and 30 November.

HMS Goliath underwent a refit at Simonstown, South Africa, from December 1914 – February 1915. When this was completed, Goliath then returned to service as flagship for Vice Admiral King Hall and resumed operations at the Rufiji River (German East Africa) until March 1915.

On 25 March 1915, Goliath was ordered to the Dardanelles to participate in the campaign there. She transferred her flag to second-class cruiser Hyacinth and departed for the Dardanelles on 1 April.[7]

On the night of 12–13 May 1915, HMS Goliath was anchored in Morto Bay, off Cape Helles, along with HMS Cornwallis and a screen of five destroyers, the weather conditions were foggy. At around 01:00 on 13 May, the Turkish torpedo boat destroyer *Muâvenet-i Millîye*, which was manned by a combined German and Turkish crew, eluded the destroyers *Beagle* and *Bulldog* and closed on the battleships. *Muâvenet-I Millîye* fired two torpedoes which struck *Goliath* almost simultaneously abreast her fore turret and abeam the fore funnel, causing a massive explosion. *Goliath* began to capsize almost immediately, and was lying on her beam ends when a third torpedo struck near her after turret. She then rolled over completely and began to sink by the bows, taking 570 of the 700-strong crew to the bottom, including her commanding officer, Captain Thomas Lawrie Shelford[8].

Amongst those who perished when the Goliath went down was Walter Thomas Mortimore, Chief Petty Officer Stoker, one of the five hundred and seventy to go down with her.

There were three other men from the South Hams area who also perished, they are Noah Robert Jonas, Stoker 1st Class, 37 years old, William T Hodge, Stoker 1st Class, and Norman Cater, Stoker 1st Class, 21, from Harberton.[9]

There is also a large plaque in Paul Parish Church, Penzance, to all the local men on board and who died on HMS Goliath. In total there are seven men from the Paul Parish named.[10]

Walter has been commemorated in St. Petroc's Church, South Brent. He, along with all the other men who died that day are also commemorated on the Plymouth Naval memorial situated on Plymouth Hoe, and in the memorial book the inscription from that book reads:

"Mortimore, Ch Sto. Number, 281426 RN. HMS Goliath, Killed in action with Turkish destroyer in Dardanelles, 13 may 1915, age 38. Husband of E.J Mortimore, The Courtlodge, Loddiswell, Devon."

Plymouth Naval Memorial on the Hoe.[11]
By permission of The Commonwealth War Graves Commission

The Commonwealth War Graves Commission inscription reads:

"War Graves Roll for 1914-1919, Born 13/1/1877, Brent, Devon, Cause of Death, Killed or died as a direct result of enemy action, Body not recovered for burial. Wife, Emma June, (Skinner) Loddiswell, Kingsbridge, Devon"

The following words were published in a Derry newspaper in memory of a Derryman, Seaman Gunner Dennis, one of the 570 men who lost their lives when the battleship Goliath was struck by torpedo's off the Dardanelles, Turkey. [12]

'In a Foreign shore he sleeps to-day
A mothers pride and joy;
He did his part with manly heart;
My brave noble boy

Chief Petty Officer Walter Thomas Mortimore was posthumously issued the 1914 Star, The British War Medal and Victory Medals.[13]

NOTES

[1] 1891 census shows Albert as a domestic servant at Kingsbridge, in 1901, age 25 at sea on HMS Highflyer, married. 1911 census he is out of the navy and shown as a Stoker at Calstock, with his wife and 5 children. Arthur died Dec. 1945 age 70 at St Germans Cornwall.

[2] 1911 census shows Fredrick Mortimore married and living in Tiverton with his family of three children, his occupation, a Compositor.

[3] 1911 census, Alice now twenty six is living and working as a servant in Newton Abbot. She dies in Newton Abbot in 1953, aged 68.

[4] 1911, Emma is shown as an apprentice dress maker in Teignmouth. The census return shows her as the niece of the household. In April 1913 Ellen now eighteen, leaves for Canada, where she is marries in March 1916 to Bartley Samuel Fultcher, in the county of Wentworth. He later joins the Canadian forces and is sent to France. He survives the war.

[5] As Goodman was her maiden name it could be assumed that John was the illegitimate child of Ellen, born before she was married when she was about eighteen. The 1881 census shows him living with Jane Goodman (55) in Bigbury Village

[6] Marine Arthur Ernest Mortimore, (grandson of William and Ellen Mortimore) Number, PLY/26647, Royal Marines HMS Exeter, 2 Feb 1945, age 41, Husband of Olive M. Mortimore, of South Brent, Devon, grave, 29 C8. Ambon War Cemetery, Indonesia. He married in 1929 to Olive M. Gunter third qtr. in Devonport. His wife lived at 6 Chapel Fields, South Brent.

[7] Burt, R. A. *British Battleships 1889–1904*. Annapolis, Maryland: Naval Institute Press, 1988, pp 158.

[8] Burt, R. A. *British Battleships 1889–1904*. Annapolis, Maryland: Naval Institute Press, 1988. P.158-59

[9] *Totnes and Mid Devon News*

[10] Information from Bob Harrison at www.paulchurch.co.uk.

[11] Courtesy of the Commonwealth War Graves Commission.

[12] www.bbc.co.uk/northernireland/radiofoyle/remembrance/goliath.

[13] National Archives, Kew, Reference Number, 1/C6783/1915.

Margaret Carew
1890 – 1918

Margret was one of the two women whose names appear on the South Brent War Memorial. She was the daughter of the Reverend Henry[1] and Maude Carew[2] , Nee Taylor[3].

The 1891 census shows the family consisted of Peter Fitzwilliam[4] aged 3 and Margret[5], 1 year old, all were residing at Church House Inn Rattery. Henry's occupation is described as *'Cleric in Holy Orders'*. There were four household staff, a children's nurse/domestic servant and three cooks/domestic servants.

The 1901 census shows Peter away at Marlborough School as a border aged 13, Margret, 11 and now a younger brother, Jasper[6] aged 6, he had been born in Rattery in 1894. The family were all now living at number 9, Powderham, in the parish of East Devon. Number 9 appears to be a lodge house, whether it was part of the Powderham estate houses for employees is not known.

The 1911 census for Margaret (21) proves interesting; at the time she was staying with John Heathworth-Amery at Knightshayes Court, Tiverton. Also staying there was Charles Carew, his wife; Muriel Carew, (nee Heathcoat-Amery) and daughter Neston aged 18. Neston was probably Margret's cousin.

It was assumed that when war broke out Margaret became a member of the Voluntary Aid Detachment, (V.A.D) but the family connection with the Amory's suggest otherwise.

It is very possible that Margaret joined the V.A.D.'s before the war. Countess Fortescue, the wife of the Lord Lieutenant, was the president of the county branch of the Red Cross, with her on the committee was Lady Amory, of Knightshayes Court, Tiverton. The Carew family were related to the Amery's and as shown earlier, Margaret was staying there in 1911.[8]

It is has now been confirmed from Margaret's Red Cross Record, that she had joined the Red Cross, V.A.D. Service in December 1914. She was working at No. 1 Section, Exeter War Hospitals, from December. 1914 onwards. At some time during the war she moved to the Coulton Hospital, Grosvenor Square, London, W1.

On her Red Cross record card, it states that she held the rank off 'Nurse', and her pay rate was '*Nil*' she was classed as a full time nurse.

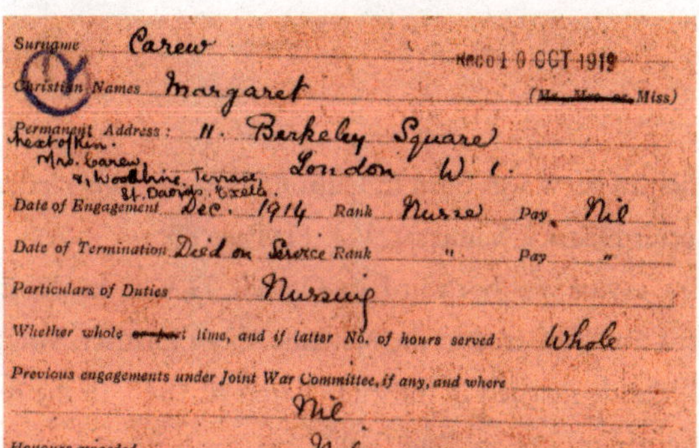
Surname Carew
REC 10 OCT 1919
Christian Names Margaret (~~Mr. Mrs. or~~ Miss)
Permanent Address: 11. Berkeley Square London W. 1.
Next of Kin: Mrs. Carew, 4, Woodbine Terrace, St. Davids, Exeter.
Date of Engagement Dec. 1914 Rank Nurse Pay Nil
Date of Termination Died on Service Rank " Pay "
Particulars of Duties Nursing
Whether whole ~~or part~~ time, and if latter No. of hours served Whole
Previous engagements under Joint War Committee, if any, and where Nil
Honours awarded Nil

Margaret's Red Cross Record Card.
Courtesy British Red Cross

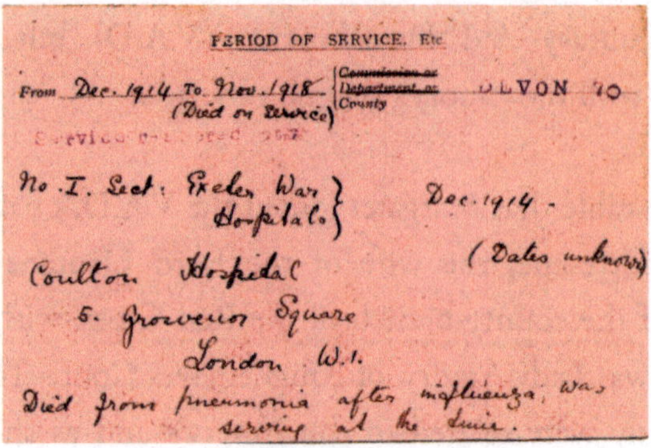

PERIOD OF SERVICE, Etc.

From Dec. 1914 To Nov. 1918 (Died on service) ~~Commission or~~ ~~Department or~~ County DEVON 40

No. I. Sect: Exeter War Hospitals — Dec. 1914.

Coulton Hospital
5. Grosvenor Square
London W.1. — (Dates unknown)

Died from pneumonia after influenza, was serving at the time.

Red Cross record card

It shows that Margaret was receiving an income from private sources, which enabled her to be able to work as a V.A.D and receive no salary. Her next of kin was her mother, Mrs Maude Carew, who was residing at 8 Woodbine Terrace, St. David's, Exeter.[9]

Margaret died from Spanish flu whilst in service with the Red Cross as a V.A.D Nurse, on the 3rd November 1918. Her death was recorded at St. George Square, London.

NOTES

1 Henry William Carew was born in Clifton, Somerset; his birth was registered in the Bedminster District, Somerset, Vol. 11. Page 85.

2 Maude Eliza Taylor was born in East Ogwell, Devon, in the 2nd quarter of 1860. Her birth was registered in the Newton Abbot District, Vol. 5b. Page 132.

3 Henry and Maude married in the 2nd quarter of 1885, in the registration district of Newton Abbot. Vol.5b. Page 249.

4 Peter Fitzwilliam Carew, born, 2nd quarter of 1887, his birth is registered in

the Totnes District, Vol.5b. Page 192. Peter married Joyce Margret Fortescue, the daughter of Lord Fortescue, Lord Lt. of Devon, in Newton Abbot, 10th April 1020. They had one son, Nicholas Jasper Grenville, who was killed in action during the Second World War. He was aged 23. Peter died in 1954, aged 66.

[5] Margaret Carew, born in Rattery, 1st quarter of 1890, the birth being registered at Totnes District, Vol. 5b. Page 193

[6] Jasper Carew was born in the 3rd quarter of 1894, the birth was registered in the Totnes District, Vol. 5b, Page, 177.

[7] The census has 'Heathworth-Amery, instead of 'Heathcoat-Amory' whether this is a spelling error on the part of the numerator is not known

[8] In May 1914, there was a big military exercise in the market towns and seaside resorts of East Devon. This exercise was run by the Royal Army Medical Corps (RAMC) in conjunction with the Red Cross and the V.A.D service. The exercise 'created' 1300 casualties, which were treated and moved to hospital by horse ambulance then train to Exeter. The exercise was deemed a great success.

[9] Red Cross record Card,

[10] Vol. 1a, Page, 972.

Mary Minnie "Polly" Rowlands, 1892 – 1918

Mary Minnie Rowlands was born in March 1892[1] to John Edmond and Susanna Rowlands, nee Brinnacombe. On the 1891 census she is shown as a five month old child. The family were living at Binnamore Farm Aish, South Brent, Devon, where her father was employed as a farm labourer.

Mary Minnie "Polly" Rowlands
From Diana Goodman archive

On the 1901 census Mary had an elder brother, John Henry who was 12 years[2], and four younger sisters. Edith 10[3] Emma, 6[4], Ada, 4[5] Florence, 2[6] and baby brother George 1[7]. Her grandfather, Richard Rowlands 69[8], was also living with the family.

The 1911 census does not show Mary who would have been about 19, living at home, she has moved out and was now living with her elder brother, John Henry, his wife Celia and two children, Mary (Minnie) is described as a visitor, single with no occupation. It is possible that her home was a little overcrowded as John, (senior) and Susanna had added to their family with three more children.

It is not known what she did between the 1911 census and the start of the war. The exact date when Mary joined the 'Woman's Army Auxiliary Corps,'[9] is not known, but it would not have been before January1917 when the W.A.A.C.'s were formed locally at Plymouth. They were then attached to the Devonshire Regiment, 3rd (Reserve) Battalion, at Devonport. Her rank was '*Worker*'[10] and her official number was 12593.

The 3rd Reserve Battalion of the Devonshire Regiment was a reserve battalion originally stationed at Exeter. It was formed on the 4th August 1914, the day hostilities were commenced.

The battalion was moved to Plymouth from Exeter on the 8th August 1914, and returned to Exeter on 28th August 1914. In May 1915 the battalion re-located again and was used for the defence of Plymouth and the military installations in the West Country. The Battalion also served as the headquarters for the Agriculture Companies, supplying men to assist on under-manned farms It also was a receiving depot for men on leave from the Mediterranean forces.

The Battalion remained in Plymouth (Devonport) throughout the war and used for administrative as well as a training facility. The Battalion finally moving to Sunderland in March 1919.

Mary died from the Spanish Flu on 5th November 1918 aged 26. The records state that she is buried in St Petroc's Church cemetery, South Brent., but I have yet to locate the grave site.

The Commonwealth War Graves Commission states that she was the daughter of 'John Edmond Rowlands and Susanna Maria Rowlands of 33 Teign Village, Hennock, Bovey Tracy'. Mary is not mentioned on either Teign Village, Hennock or Bovey Tracy war memorials.

The photo of Mary, at the beginning of this piece was the last photo of her which was received in the mail by Celia Rowlands in the autumn of 1918. On the back Mary, known as Polly in the family wrote:

Dear All, Most likely I shall be out on Thursday by myself.

The post card sent to Celia was in an envelope and un-franked, so where it was sent from or to is not known, but there is a good chance that it sent from Devonport (where Minnie was stationed) to Plympton St Mary, to her sister in law, where Celia was living. The phrase used 'I *most likely shall be out'* could refer to either her visiting her sister in law on Thursday or to her being discharge from hospital on Thursday. We shall never know.

Celia's husband John died in September 1915 and she re-marries in the first quarter of 1919 to Robert Mc Micken at Plympton. The family then moved firstly to Canada then to North America in 1920. They are all recorded as entering the United States at the Michigan border control on the 20th September 1920. (See John Henry Rowlands, Chapter 4.)

NOTES

[1] Totnes District, First Quarter 1892, Vol. 5b.Page 186.

[2] See Private John Henry Rowlands.

[3] Edith Rowlands, 1891-1963, Married Stanley Pettyjohns in 1920, Died in Kent

[4] Emma Rowlands, 1894-1997, Married Charles Hind, in 1917, died aged 103 in the Taunton Area.

[5] Ada Rowlands, 1908- Unknown.

[6] Florence Rowlands, 1899-unknown

[7] George Rowlands, 1900-1983, married Catherine Willis, 1926, Newton Abbot

[8] Richard Rowlands, 1832-1909

[9] The United Kingdom's Women's Army Auxiliary Corps (1917–1918) was later re-named Queen Mary's Army Auxiliary Corps (1918–1920). Over 57,000 women served between January 1917 and November 1918. On 31 March 1917 women in the W.A.A.C were first sent to the battlefields in France,

[10] Women in the W.A.A.C were not given full military status. They enrolled rather than enlisted. Women in the W.A.A.C were divided into officials (officers), fore-women (sergeant), assistant forewomen (corporals) and workers (privates).

Ernest William Bishop
1895 – 1917

Born in South Brent, Ernest was the second child of Henry and Mary Agnes[1] (nee Lang) Bishop. His elder brother was George 9[2], with younger sisters Caroline 5[3], Florence 3[4] and baby brother Sydney nine months[5]. On the 1901 census the family was living at Lutton Cottages, South Brent. Henry Bishop (father) was employed as an agriculture labourer, Mary, housewife. By the time the 1911 census was taken there was another brother, Percy.[6]

The 1911 census shows the older children working, George was a farm labourer, Ernest a horse driver and coal merchant and Caroline in domestic service. The younger children were at school in the village. The census also notes that there was a child born who had died and the Bishop's had been married for 22 years. They were still residing at number 3, Lutton Cottages.

The Bishop family was related through marriage to the Lang's of South Brent. Ernest William Bishop was the first cousin to Jarvis Lang mentioned later in this work. Ernest's mother's maiden name was Lang, Ernest and Jarvis shared the same grandparents.

In 1913 Ernest left these shores for Canada, sailing on the 23rd of April, destination Quebec. He was not alone, with him went three other men from the Totnes/South Brent area, Arthur Baskerville, John Hannaford and Arthur Teans or Terns. They travelled third class and sailed from Southampton. The ship was the SS Ultonia belonging to the Cunard shipping line.

It is not known when exactly Ernest joined the Canadian Army. The history indicates that he may have joined up in the later part of 1914 at Valcartier in Quebec. Two thirds of the men who joined up in this first wave were born in the United Kingdom. From the Canadian military records, Ernest was in the 5th Battalion; (Western Cavalry)[7] the Canadian Infantry, Saskatchewan Regiment, formed on the 6th August 1914, and Ernest's official number was A/24106.

All the various battalions of the Canadian Expeditionary Force (C.E.F) wore a coloured sleeve badges with various geometric symbols indicating the individual battalion's.[8] The cap badge worn by the Canadian was the basic Maple Leaf. Specialist units were indicated by having various insignia place in or around the basic design.

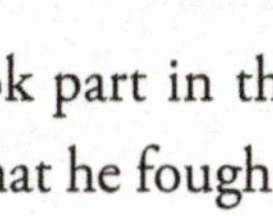

Sleeve badge

It is known that Ernest took part in the 'The Arras Offensive' (9th April-16h June 1917) and that he fought at Vimy Ridge, also known as 'Hill 145'[9]. This action commenced on the 9th April and lasted until the 14th.[10]

The attack was due to begin at 5:30 am on Easter Monday, 9th April 1917. The attack had been originally planned for the morning of 8th April (Easter Sunday), but it was postponed for 24 hours at the request of the French.[11] During the late hours of 8th April and early morning of the 9th April the men of the leading and supporting wave of the attack were moved into their forward assembly positions. The weather was cold and later changed to sleet and snow[12].

At exactly 5:30 am on the 9th April every artillery piece at the disposal of the Canadian Corps began firing. Thirty seconds later, engineers detonated the mine charges laid under no man's land and the German trench line, destroying a number of German strong points and creating secure communication trenches directly across no man's land. Light field guns laid down a barrage that advanced in predetermined increments, often 100 yards every three minutes, while medium and heavy howitzers established a series of standing barrages further ahead, against known defensive systems.[14]

During the early fighting the German divisional artilleries, despite heavy losses, were able to maintain their defensive firing.[15] As the Canadian assault advanced, they overran many of the German guns because there was no means of the Germans moving them to the rear on account of many of the horses being killed in the initial gas attack.[16]

The 1st, 2nd and 3rd Canadian Divisions reported reaching and capturing their first objective, the Black Line, by 6:25 am.[17] The 4th

Canadian Division encountered a great deal of trouble during its advance and was unable to complete its first objective until some hours later.[18] After a planned pause, when the 1st, 2nd and 3rd Canadian Divisions consolidated their positions, the advance resumed. Shortly after 7:00 am, the 1st Canadian Division captured the left half of its second objective, the Red Line, and moved the 1st Canadian Brigade forward to mount an attack on the remainder.[19] The 2nd Canadian Division reported reaching the Red Line and capturing the town of Les Tilleuls at approximately the same time.[20]

It was sometime after the main attack that Ernest was killed, The Totnes and Mid Devon News reported on the 5th May 1917 that Ernest had been killed at Vimy Ridge. The article read-:

South Brent.

'The relatives of Pte. Ernest Bishop have received unofficial information that their second son, serving with the Canadians in France was killed in the Vimy Ridge battle. Pte. Bishop was a fine soldier, well known in Brent, where his parents reside. Information indicates that he escaped injury in the actual engagement but was picked off subsequently. Muffled peals were rung at the Church on Sunday and Monday'.[21]

Private Ernest William Bishop is buried in Plot 1V. A15 at the Nine Elms Military Cemetery, Thelus in Northern France. The cemetery was begun, after the capture of Vimy Ridge, by the burial in what is now Plot I, Row A of 80 men of the 14th Canadian Infantry Battalion, who fell on the 9th April 1917.

Three burials were made in Plot I, Row C, in July 1918. The rest of the cemetery was made after the Armistice by the concentration of British and French graves from the battlefields of Vimy and Neuville-St. Vaast.[22]

The Canadian Memorial on Vimy Ridge
(The view from Hill 145, Author's collection)

Looking at the Canadian army form regarding Ernest's burial, it appears that he was buried twice before finally being laid to rest at the Nine Elms Cemetery.

It is not known what medals Ernest was awarded but there is a very good possibility that his mother would have been sent the Memorial Cross also known as the silver cross. This was created in 1919 and was issued to the mothers and widows of Canadian military personal who died in service.

The Canadian Silver Cross.

NOTES

[1] Mary Agnes Lang was born in the 3rd quarter of 1863, Totnes District Vol. 5b, Page 176.

[2] George was born in 1892

[3] Caroline was born in the 1st quarter of 1896, Totnes District, Vol. 5b. Page 173.

[4] Florence was born in 1898

[5] Sydney was born in the 3rd quarter of 1900, (26th June 1900) Totnes District, Vol. 5b, Page 148. He died in September 1974, age 74, Plymouth District, Vol. 21, Page 1857.

[6] Percy was born in the 4th quarter of 1904, Totnes District Vol. 5b, Page 151.

[7] The 5th Battalion (Western Cavalry), C.E.F, was authorized on 10 August 1914 and embarked for Great Britain on 29 September 1915. It entered the theatre of operations in France on 14 February 1915, where it fought as part of the 2nd Infantry Brigade, 1st Canadian Division in France and Flanders until the end of the war.

[8] The full story of the evolution of Canadian formation patches, or "battle patches" is given in Clive Law's book *"Distinguishing Patches"* available from Service Publications.

[9] Hill 154 is now a 250 acre portion of the former battleground which serves as a preserved memorial park and site of the Canadian Nationals.

[10] Historians attribute the success of the Canadian Corps in capturing the ridge to a mixture of technical and tactical innovation, meticulous planning, powerful

artillery support and extensive training as well as the failure of the German Sixth Army to properly apply the new German defensive doctrine. The battle was the first occasion when all four divisions of the Canadian Expeditionary Force participated in a battle together.

[11] McGill, Harold W. (2007), Norris, Marjorie, ed., *Medicine and duty: the World War I memoir of Captain Harold W. McGill, Medical Officer, 31st Battalion, C.E.F*, P.261.

[12] Turner, Alexander (2005), *Vimy Ridge 1917: Byng's Canadians Triumph at Arras,* P 52

[13] Rawling, Bill (2007) "The Sappers of Vimy: Specialized Support for the Assault of 9 April 1917" in Hayes, Geoffrey, Iarocci, Andrew; Bechthold, Mike, *Vimy Ridge: A Canadian Reassessment, Waterloo:* Wilfred Laurier University. P.131-133.

[14] Cook, Tim (2007), *"The Gunners of Vimy Ridge:* 'We are Hammering Fritz to Pieces' P.117

[15] Sheldon, Jack (2008), *The German Army on Vimy Ridge 1914–1917*, Barnsley (UK): Pen & Sword Military, P.298

[16] Ibid; P.299

[17] Nicholson, G. W. L. (1967), *The Gunners of Canada – The History of the Royal Regiment of Canadian Artillery, Volume 1, 1534–1919*, P. 254

[18] Ibid; P.254

[19] Ibid; p 255

[20] Campbell, David (2007), *"The 2nd Canadian Division: A 'Most Spectacular Battle'"*, in Hayes, Geoffrey; Iarocci, Andrew; Bechthold, Mike, *Vimy Ridge: A Canadian Reassessment*, Waterloo: Wilfrid Laurier University Press. P

[21] *Totnes and Mid Devon News*, 5th May 1917.

[22] Information from the Commonwealth War Graves Commission web site.

Chapter Three

The names of the Serviceman from South Brent who are not on the War Memorial in St Petroc's Church

Pte. Alfred John Goss. 27323.
Duke of Cornwall's Light Infantry.

Pte. Fredrick Hall, 3145.
2/6th Devon Regiment.

Chief Stoker F. Joint. RN. 276316
HMS Cornwall.

Pte. Jarvis Lang. 2010.
5th (Prince of Wales) Devon's.

Gnr. J.H. Rowlands. 275.
Royal Garrison Artillery.

Alfred John Goss (27323)
1889 – 1916

Alfred John Goss[1] was the first son, second child of William Henry[2] and Mary Grace Goss, (nee Full) born in 1889. His elder sister was Ethel[3] and his younger one Nora Bessie[4]. The family was from Rattery, Devon.

The 1901census is the first time Alfred appears, (there is no trace of the family for the 1891 census) when he is 11 and still at school. The family was living at Higher Velwell, Rattery at the time of this census.

On the 1911 census he is aged 22 and is shown as an agriculture labourer working with his father, William at Sunnyside, Staverton, Totnes. His sister, Ethel was a self-employed dressmaker working from home. Nora is absent from the family return, but is shown working and living in Paignton as a domestic housemaid.

Alfred John Goss. (27323)
Photo courtesy Totnes Photo Bank

Alfred enlisted at Newton Abbot with the 7th (Service) Battalion; Duke of Cornwall's Light Infantry (DCLI) and was given the number 27323. His number indicates that he joined up after December 1915.[5]

Alfred would have fought as part of the 4th Army in the Battle of Deville Wood, one of the phases of the first Somme offensive, under Rawlinson. This action took place between the 15th August and the 3rd September 1916. This led to the battle of Guillemont (3rd – 6th Sept 1916)

It was in this battle that Alfred was killed on the 6th September 1916, aged 27. He has no known grave and is commemorated on the Theipval memorial.

Theipval memorial
Photo: Author

His name in inscribed on pier and face 6b and the Totnes memorial.

Alfred was awarded the Victory and British War Medals. Alfred left a wife Mabel Jane, who was residing at 6 Cistern Street, Totnes.

I have included Alfred John Goss in this work because of the family connection with Rattery, and the fact that Edwin Goss (his uncle) is mentioned on the war memorial of South Brent, (which I think is incorrect). It is also worth noting that the 7th (Service) Battalion of the DCLI was the service battalion of *'The Last Tommy'* Harry Patch.

Harry Patch on a visit to Talbert House, Belgium

NOTES

1 Alfred John Goss was born in the 4th quarter of 1889 and registered in the Totnes District, Vol. 5b.Page, 189.

2 William Goss was born in 1862 at Rattery. He married Mary Grace Full, from Buckfastleigh in the 1st quarter of 1887 the marriage was registered in the Totnes District, Vol. 5b. Page 253

3 Nora Bessie Goss was born in the 2nd quarter of 1894 in Rattery. The birth was registered at Totnes, Vol. 5b. Page, 171.

4 The 7th Service Battalion was originally formed in Bodmin in September 1914 (K2) moved to Aldershot and came under the command of the 61st Brigade, 20th

Light Division. In February 1915 they moved to Witley and moved again in March 1915 to Amesbury. The battalion was mobilised to France on the 25th July 1915 and landed at Boulogne. By the 26th July the 20th division was complete and were concentrated in the Saint- Omar area from where they were engaged in various actions.

[5] www.hargreave-mawson.demon.co.uk/DCLI

Fredrick Hall
1895 – 1916

Fred was born in South Brent in 1895 and first appears on the 1901 census. This states that the family is living in Horsebrook, South Brent where his brothers, Walter, Fredrick and Charles, were seven, six and five respectfully. Richard Hall (father) was occupied as an Agriculture labourer born in Ugborough. His wife, Sarah was born in North Huish; all the boys were born in South Brent. There were also two elder daughters, Beatrice (12) and Annie (10).

The 1911 census return shows just the three boys and a younger sister, Ethel (8). Walter and Charles are employed as gardeners, Fredrick, a groom and helper in the garden. Beatrice and Annie are not shown on any family records after 1901. The census also states that Richard and Sarah had been married for twenty two years and had seven children of which one had died.

Fred, official number 3145, later changed to 266411, enlisted with the 2/6th Battalion Territorial Force, The Devon Regiment at Totnes, Devon, the date is unknown, but the probability is as soon as war was declared

The 2nd/6th battalion along with the 2nd/4th battalion sailed for India at the end of December 1914 arriving at Bombay in January 1915. The 2nd/4th proceeded to Wellington in the Madras, the 2/6th remained in Bombay. In February 1915, after the departure of these units for India, all the military documentation was collated at Tavistock, where the name 'The Devon and Cornwall Brigade, Provisional Battalion' was conferred upon these battalions.

In March 1916, the 2nd/6th was moved to Chakrata then later on to Peshawar. It is thought that Fred was now with the 6th Battalion of the Devon's who were on their way to try and relieve Kut.

The official history states that "*The first relief expedition comprised some 19,000 men under General Aylmerand it headed up the river from Ali Gharbi in January 1916. He had been reinforced with another division, the 13th (Western) Division. The next month was spent resting the troops and probing the Ottoman defensive positions. With time running out on General Townshend's garrison in Kut*"

General Aylmerand finally launched a two pronged attack on the Ottoman positions, one attack at the Sinn Abtar Redoubt, the other attack at the Dujaila Redoubt. The attacks were launched on 7 March 1916. Both attacks failed due to lack of initiative and an inability to coordinate the timing of the assaults (they ended up being sequential, not simultaneous). The British had some 4,000 casualties.[1]

Fred was not one of the causalities. The Totnes and Mid Devon News of 2nd September 1916 printed a short article under the headline:

"South Brent"
It was officially reported that Private F. Hall 3145, of the Devon Regiment been taken prisoner at Kut-El-Amara.

One week later the paper printed the following:

"Private Fred Hall, second son, of Mr and Mrs Richard Hall of South Brent, with the Royal Kent regiment, after engaging in the Mesopotamia campaign was sent to General Townshead expedition to the relief of Kut. He with the remainder of the besieged forces who only surrendered after a protracted and exhausting siege, he was taken prisoner by the Turks and is now interned at Adana, in Turkey".[2]

Adana was a prison hospital/camp where many British and Indian soldiers died of disease. Fred was one, he died of Malaria on the 22nd September 1916, aged 22. He was buried locally and at the end of the war a lot of the allied prisoners who had died were exhumed and re-buried at Bagdad (North Wall Gate) cemetery. (Grave XXI Q36)

There is some doubt that Fred was actually in the Royal Kent Regiment, as stated in the Totnes Times, It appears he was attached to the 2nd Battalion, Royal West Kent Regiment. Which was in itself attached to the 30th Brigade, 6th (Poona) Division in November 1915. They became besieged at Kut-al-Amara and were captured on the 29th April 1916.

The medal records for Fred only show him in the 2nd/6th Devons. His service number is shown on the medal record card as 3145, yet on the official document listing the names of the men buried in the North Gate Cemetery in Iraq, he is shown as 266411. It can only be assumed that his first number was issued to him as he was a member of the Territorial Force prior to being enlisted into Kitchener's army when territorial numbers were replaced with "official" numbers. The history of the Devon regiment by L.T. Atkinson, show him as having the number 266411.

Fred was awarded the British War Medal, the Victory Medal and the 1915 Star.

North Huish Church Memorial

Private Fredrick Hall is also commemorated on the war memorial of North Huish Church, Devon.

The official citation in the Commonwealth War Graves register reads:

Hall, Pte. Fredrick.3145, 2nd/6th Batt. Devon Regt. died of malaria whilst a prisoner of war 22nd sept. 1916 age 22. Son of Richard Foster Hall and Sarah Jane Hall of Avonwick, South Devon. (Grave XX1 Q36)

In a large article published in the Totnes and Mid Devon News in May 1916 the headline reads:

"Avonwick Soldiers",

The three sons of Mr and Mrs Richard Hall of Avonwick, after bravely fighting for their country, are now by the fortunes of war incapacitated for further service in this titanic struggle of nations. The eldest, Gunner Walter Hall after passing 12 months in the Royal Garrison Artillery, at Plymouth joined the Heavy Siege Battery and was dispatched to Lydd, Kent for heavy siege drill. After completing the necessary exercises he was drafted to Egypt where he stayed for three months preceding eventually to France, continually sustaining his part in the operation of the guns of the heaviest calibre

He is now at home after treatment for shell shock at St Mary's Hospital Paddington.

Pvt. Fred Hall, second son, of the Royal Kent Regt, after engaging in the Mesopotamia campaign was sent to General Townshend's expedition to the relief of Kut. Here with the remainder of the besieged forces who only surrendered after a protracted and exhausting siege, he was taken prisoner of war by the Turks and is now interned at Adana, in Turkey.

Pvt. Charles hall, 3 of the 3rd Devon's has seen five months service in France. During the great advance in July on the Western front he received five severe wounds and lay for three days in a shell pit. He is now laying in a military hospital at Leicester where he is still suffering from the extradition of fragments of bone.

Thus England continues to give the bravest and best of her sons to the gigantic conflict.

NOTES

[1] In the historical context, the city finally fell in March 1916, but the position was not fully consolidated until the end of April. General Townshend arranged a ceasefire on the 26th April 1916 and, after failed negotiations, he simply surrendered on 29 April 1916 after a siege of 147 days. Around 13,000 Allied soldiers survived to be made prisoners. 70% of the British and 50% of the Indian troops died of disease or at the hands of their Ottoman guards during captivity.

[2] H. C. W. Bishop has written a very descriptive book entitled *"A Kut Prisoner"* available on the internet as an eBook.

[3] Totnes and Mid Devon News

[4] The 2nd /6th Battalion of the Devon Regiment was a territorial force formed in September 1914 at Barnstable as part of the second Devon and Cornwall Brigade.

Fredrick Joint
1875 – 1915

Fredrick Joint was the fifth son of Henry (1837-1903) and Elizabeth nee Knapman[1] Joint, (1839-1913) and was born in South Brent in 1875.[2] His father was an agriculture labourer, the family resided at 6 Higher Cheston, South Brent.

The family is shown on the 1881 census as having seven children, the eldest son being Henry (1858-1921) a Block Layer[3], Andrew (1860-1937) a Farm Labourer[4] John (1871-1937) Mary Ann (8), Fred (6), Charles (4) are all at school and Sarah Ann (1).

Fred does not appear on the 1891 census at the family home so one has to assume that as he was a seaman with the Royal Navy or he was in a boys training establishment. He appears on the 1901 census, aged 26, in the Royal Navy as a crew member of HMS Hood[5] in the Grand Harbour, Valletta, Malta. His occupation is described as a Stoker.

On the 1911 census he has now married to Emma Jane Bowhay , from Blackawton, Devon,[7] they have two sons, Fredrick and William. There is also a lodger staying with the family, James Crocker aged 76, a widower.

On the 19th March 1913, Fred was awarded the Naval Good Conduct Medal; He is listed as a Petty Officer serving on board HMS Cornwall. He received his award on 13th May 1913.

The ships log book for HMS Cornwall of the 30th March 1915 shows that at:

'*1025, (hours) Chief Stoker Fredrick Joint No. 276316, departed this life.*'

Later the same day, the ships log records that at:

5:5, (hours) ship stopped, held the service for burial a sea for Chief Stoker Fredrick Joint,

5:30, proceeded underway rev.120.

On the Plymouth Naval Memorial on the Hoe, the index (2) it reads:

Joint, Ch. Sto. Fredrick, 276316. R N HMS Cornwall, died of pneumonia 30th March 1915, age 40. Son of Henry and Elizabeth Joint of South Brent Devon; husband of Emma Jane Joint of Blackawton, Totnes Devon

As well as the Naval Memorial on Plymouth Hoe, Fred is also remembered on the memorial at Blackawton.

The War Memorial in the main Street, Blackawton.

It is worth mentioning that Fred's elder brother Henry (1858-1921) had six children. Henry's fourth child was named **Archie Joint.**

In the 1911 census Archie was a servant at Kerrydowns, South Brent, working horses on the farm of Mr Henry Joint, who being too old to be called up for service in the first war. His son Archie was not. He joined the 9th Service Battalion of the Devon Regiment, which was formed at Exeter in September 1914. It was part Kitchener's army and was attached to the 20th Light Division.

They left the division in July 1915 and joined the 20th Brigade, 7th Division and landed at Le Havre in July. When Archie actually joined the 20th Brigade is not known. He took part in the first phase of the Battle of the Somme, the Battle of Albert (1-13 July 1916) and the capture of Mametz. It was during this battle that Archie was killed.

He has no known grave and is remembered on the Theipval Memorial.

The Theipval Memorial
Photo: Author

Archie is also remembered on the Rattery War Memorial at the entrance to the Church yard.

Private A. Joint. 16651; Devon Regiment.
Killed in Action, 1st July 1916.

Another of Fred's brother's was a career serviceman. **Charles Joint** joined the Royal Navy as a stoker and is shown on the 1911 census as Chief Petty Officer Stoker, at the Naval Base Portland. He was awarded a clasp for service in the Persian Gulf in 1915 and a long service medal in 1922. He died in 1924, aged 47.

The youngest of Fred's brother's was **Richard Joint,** he survived the war and went on to live for a long time, dying in 1952. He was awarded the Military Medal for bravery under fire during the Great War

NOTES

[1] Married 2nd Quarter 1857, Totnes District, Vol. 5b, Page 284.

[2] 3rd Quarter 1874, Totnes District, Vol.5b, Page 192.(28/11/1874)

[3] Henry married Sarah Pullybank, from Modbury.

[4] Andrew married Mary Jane Rider, Plympton St Mary District, Vol. 5b, Page 355

[5] HMS Hood was a modified *Royal Sovereign*-class pre-dreadnought battleship built for the Royal Navy in the early 1890s and the last of the eight built. She differed from the other ships of the class in that she had cylindrical gun turrets instead of barbettes and a lower freeboard. She served most of her active career in the Mediterranean Sea.

[6] Emma died in June 1963, aged 86, Totnes District, vol.7a p866.

[7] Married 2nd Quarter 1903, Kingsbridge District, Vol.5b, Page 463

Jarvis Henry Lang
1890 – 1916

Jarvis Lang is another of the lads from South Brent who is not remembered on the Church memorial, why is not known but it is hoped that the matter can be rectified.

He was the only child of James and Mary Lang and was born in South Brent in the third quarter of 1890.[1] The family lived at Didworthy where his father was a farm labourer. The 1891census shows Jarvis as a seven month old baby.

In 1901 the census has Jarvis as a ten year old scholar, his father was also called Jarvis, living with them is his grandfather also Jarvis, he dies in 1908. By 1911, Jarvis (snr) and Mary had been married 21 years. The family was now living at Bloomfield House, Brent Mill, South Brent. Jarvis Jnr. is 20 and working as a chauffeur, while his father remained as an agriculture labourer.

When war broke out, Jarvis was one of the first to join up. He was attested at Exeter in August 1914.[2] His service document shows that he commenced service on the 5th August 1914. According to his service records of 1914, he was now living at Two Bridges, Princetown.

There is a mis-spelling of his name, it has been written badly but reads **'Jawis'**. He enlisted in the 5th (Prince of Wales) Battalion, TA.

Devon Regiment and his official number was 2010.The unit moved from Exeter to Plymouth in August 1914 and then to Salisbury Plain.

On the 8th October 1914, the 1st/5th was sent to India[3] landing at Karachi on the 11th November 1914. On arrival the 5th were sent to Multan. Multan was one of the hottest and dustiest areas of India. The regiment was attached to the 3rd (Lahore) Division area at Multan. The division left for Lahore in December 1915. A notation on his army record states that Jarvis had '*Died at station hospital Lahore of endemic fever. 9/6/1916*'

Jarvis served in the UK from 5th Aug-9th Oct. 14, a total of 65 days, and from 8th Oct – 9/6/16, 245 days in India. He was awarded The British War Medal.

It is not known where Jarvis Lang is actually buried; his name has been inscribed on the Karachi (Pakistan) 1914-1918 War Memorial.

There is also a letter from the War Office to his next of kin requesting instructions on the disposal of the personal effects of the late Jarvis Lang. It is dated 12/1/1917.

His next of kin were his parents, who had now moved from South Brent to Newton Abbot. His father, Jarvis (Snr) acknowledges receipt of his war medals, and in May 1919, the Officer in Charge of the Devonshire Regiment records office, at Exeter sent instructions of how to claim the memorial plaque (The Death Penny) to Mrs Lang, at Newton Abbot.

It is worth noting that there were other men from the Lang family who had enlisted. They returned home after the war and are listed under 'Other Brent Men'

NOTES

[1] Totnes District, Vol. 5b. Page 161

[2] There seems to be some confusion as to where he joined up. His documents have Exeter on them but the book on the Devon's by C .T. Atkinson has him enlisting at Plymouth.

[3] The 4th and 5th Devon's embarked on to the Nevasa, the 6th on the Galeka, both transport ships. In all they made up the Wessex Division, totalling 99 officers and 2,404 men. The 5th had 28 officers and 800 men.

[4] Mother, residing in what looks like '151 Lucian St', Newton Abbott.

John Henry Rowlands
1889-1915

John Henry Rowlands was the first born son of John Edmond and Susanna Maria, nee Brimicombe Rowlands.

John was born in 1889 in the village of South Kingston, Devon. On the 1891 census he is two years old and living in Aish village, South Brent. He also has a younger sister, Edith[1], who is nine months old also born in Aish Village. John's father's occupation was an agriculture labourer working in Aish village.

According to the 1911 census, John's parents went on to have a further four daughters and two sons. It is noted that John's grandfather worked at South Brent Flock Mill. (It is thought that the mill was situated at Millswood.)

There is no trace of the family for the 1901 census date, the reason for this is not known, but they all appear in the 1911 census.

The national census for 1911 now shows John to be married and living at Aish Cottages, South Brent, with his wife Celia, nee Elliott age 21, whom he married in 1908 at Totnes. They have two children, Gladys Lilian Florence[2], (2) and George Henry[3], eleven months.[4] John's occupation is given as a Plate Layer with the Great Western Railway.

Also living with John and his family at the time of the census was his sister, Mary Minnie Rowlands, described as a visitor. At the time Minnie was 19 years old, single. Her occupation is not given.

Some when between the 1911 census and 1913, John Rowlands and the family left South Brent and moved to Plympton and he was now working in the China clay industry. John joined the Territorial Army on the 11th December 1913 at Plympton, and states on his entry documents he is from South Brent, Devon, aged 24 and married.

On his initial medical record he is aged 25, in good health and with good vision. The Army Medical was carried out on the 2nd December 1913 and signed by C. Stevens, Medical Officer. He is certified fit to serve in the Devonshire Royal Garrison Artillery (R.G.A) by Capt. Andrews at Plympton on the 13th December 1913. John is issued with an official number, 275 and listed as a gunner.

The Army document show he is posted to Ashtead (Surrey) to join the 2nd Heavy Battery on the 11th December 1913 and remains there until 11th December 1914, when he was then discharged as unfit for service.

The Medical Officer's report at the time gives a diagnosis of Tuberculosis, and is given as the reason for his discharge from the army. The report states that the disease was acquired at Codford Fort (Salisbury Plain) in October 1914.

There is a lot of written argument on the medical report as to whether John was entitled to an army pension. In April 1915, the Director General Army Medical Services (DGAMS) states that:

'*this man cannot be regarded for pension purposes*'.

In the July of the same year, the DGAMS writes that:

'*The man's present condition cannot be regarded as due to service*'.

In March 1917, there has been a note added, it reads:

'*This man died on the 23rd September 1915, and the widow is now applying for pension*'

On the 20th April 1917, the DGAMS recants and writes:

'*This man's recent condition may be regarded as acquired in service in the view of fresh evidence. Man is reported to have died 23rd September 1915*'.

It appears that the army medical establishment did not want to be seen as having missed John's illness. A medical certificate was issued stating that John was in good health and at work up to the time he was joined the TA's at Plympton.

As stated John Henry Rowlands died on the 23rd September 1915, he was 26 years old. His death was registered at Plympton St Mary, (Volume 5b. P.229.) He is buried in the Churchyard of Plympton St Mary's church.

Celia , his widow, re-married in 1919 to Robert McMichen, an Irishman, in Devon and left England for Canada. They had two more children, William and Dorothy.

On the 20th September 1920, they [the family] are recorded as having entered the United States of America via Michigan. Gladys was 11 at the time and is recorded as Irish, when in fact she is English and the daughter of John Henry Rowlands. Celia moved on to Wisconsin and died in 1940.

John and Celia had in all four children of which two are mentioned. After 1911, Celia and John had Dorothy and William (Bill). This information was obtained from the Great niece of John Henry Rowlands

---

NOTES

[1] Edith Annie was born in the 3rd quarter of 1890, Totnes District, Vol. 5b. Page 183. She

[2] Gladys Lillian Florence Rowland was born in the 2nd quarter of 1909, registered in the Totnes District, Vol. 5b. Page161. She immigrated with her mother to Canada and crossed into the United States of America on the 23rd September 1920. Her nationality is shown as Irish. This is wrong as her mother re-married an Irish national, it may have been easier to enter the USA.

[3] George Henry Rowland was born in 1st quarter of 1910 and registered in the Totnes District, Vol. 5b. Page 150. He died in April 1995, aged 86 and his death is registered in Plymouth. It interesting to note that the date of birth is given as 8th Feb.1909. It should be 1910, as his sister was born after him!

[4] At the time of writing this was the most up to date information available. I have since heard from Diane Goodman (in the USA) the great granddaughter of Gladys, informing me that there were an additional two children, Dorothy and Bill. Dorothy died in June 2013.

[5] Celia Rowlands, Photo courtesy of Diana Goodman Archive

Chapter Four

The two Serviceman who are not from South Brent and are buried in the Cemetery of St Petroc's Church

Pvt. Benjamin Harold Cook

1st/4th Battalion

Duke of Cornwall's Light Infantry

Pvt. Arthur William Parsons,

1st/4th Battalion

Duke of Cornwall's Light Infantry

No. 23 Prot. Royal Defence Corps

Benjamin Harold Cook
1894 – 1916

Benjamin came to South Brent as a civilian having been discharged from the army medically unfit.

Benjamin joined the 1st/4th Battalion, Duke of Cornwall's Light Infantry, having his first medical in Truro on 3rd September 1914. On his army application form his second Christian name 'Harold' has been omitted, who did this and why is not known. His service record shows that he was at the home station from 3rd September 1914 until 8th October. On the 9th October he was sent with the regiment to India, as part of the Wessex Division. He remained in India until 30th May 1916 when he was sent home and discharged from the army. His army service was terminated on medical grounds on the 4th July 1916.

The statement of service record has two entries only, his initial entry details into the army, rank and dates of service. The second entry dated 1st July 1916 States;

"*Discharged no longer fit for war service Para 392 XV1 Kings Regulations*".

A total service 306 days service.

This lower section reads:

"*The discharge of the above named is hereby approved*"

Station, Exeter 4th July 1916. Signed (unreadable)

The medical report on Benjamin is sad reading. Apart from his basic details, height weight, age and home address the comments on the lower half are as follows; –

"*Cause of discharge, medically unfit, Tuberculous of the lung*".

Date12.6.1916. Originated in India June 1916. Enlisted in Sept. 1914 at which time he was quite fit.

The last line of the medical report reads:

"*Fatal at present ¼ – 6/12 (1-6 months life expectancy) if placed under suitable treatment*".

Benjamin was sent to Didworthy Sanatorium by the Cornwall Insurance Commission and was admitted on 5th July 1916. Information from the Didworthy Sanatorium admission register:

Benjamin Harold Cook of 31 Richmond Hill, Truro, noted as invalided soldier, age 22, single, and noted that the disease first developed October 1915 and possibly before that.

He died at Didworthy on the 15th July 1916. His death was registered at Totnes, on September 1916, Vol. 5b. Page 195.

Benjamin was 23 years old and is buried in the cemetery at South Brent. The funeral was carried out by Mr A.W. Cranch and Co. of South Brent. The headstone was provided by the war graves commission. Benjamin's name also appears on the Truro War Memorial in the city.

Private B. H. Cooke 2069
Duke of Cornwall's Light Infantry.
15th July 1916 Age 22
Photo: Author's collection

Truro War Memorial.
Photo courtesy Bob Harris.

Arthur William Parsons, 1890 – 1916

From what little information gleaned Arthur was born in Salcombe in 1890 to Edmund and Margaret Parsons. He was the youngest of five children, Julia 7, Edward 5, Alfred 4, Margaret 2 and Arthur 3 months. His father and mother both came originally from Guernsey

In the 1891 census the family were all resident in Salcombe, where Arthur was born. His older brothers and sisters were born in Scotland. The occupation of Edmund Parsons, their father was that of a Coast Guard and the family were now living at 16 Robinsons Row, Salcombe Devon.

Arthur next appears on the 1901 census aged 10 and at school in Dorset. His father is now the Chief Boatman Coast Guard residing at Number 1, Coast Guard Station, Portland Dorset. Both of his brothers, Edward and Alfred, are missing from this census. Arthur does not appear on the 1911 census, where he is, is a mystery.

From the army records, it is known that he was attested for Number 3, Super Numery Company, Territorial Force, DCLI, signing for one year service in the United Kingdom, on the 19th October 1914. His attestment form shows two other service numbers, 20478 and 3371, these have been crossed out and the final number of 7390 issued. There is also a notation that Arthur has served in the Royal Garrison Artillery as a reservist.

There is a an amendment, in pen stating that he will serve for the period of the war and only be discharged if the war ends within one year, to which he agrees. He signed this form in front of the magistrate at St Just on the 19th October 1914. According to his discharge papers, Arthur's occupation before joining the army was a Clay Worker.

Arthur was medically examined on the 17th February 1914 and signed fit for service by R. Nesbitt, Medical Officer. The medical was carried out at St Austell. It is worth noting that the medical officer has certified that Arthur is not suffering from any of the various ailments listed including chest infection.

The Certificate of the approving officer, on the bottom of the attestment form has assigned Arthur to No. 3 Railway Company, 4th DCLI. The approving officer is Captain W. A. Pollack, 4th DCLI.

The 1st/4th Battalion was a territorial force formed in Truro in August 1914 it was part of the Devon and Cornwall Brigade, on mobilisation the brigade was moved from Truro to Falmouth, at the end of August 1914 the brigade was moved to Perham Down, on Salisbury Plain. On the 9th October 1914 the brigade sailed for India, as part of the Wessex Division, arriving at Bombay on the 10 November 1914.

The battalion's duties in India was mainly Internal Security, looking after British interests. This allowed the regular army soldiers to be sent to France to supplement the main forces on the Western front.

As Arthur joined the DCLI on the 19th October 1914, ten days after the 1st/4th had sailed for India. Where he worked and what he did is not known. His army records do not indicate anything. The only notation made is on the 26th April 1916. Here he was transferred to the Royal Defence Corps. This transfer implies that he was not fit enough for a full active service in the army.

On his medical notes of 1st August 1916, it states that he first presented with a chest infection in May 1915. He was diagnosed with either Pleurisy or Phenomena. The last line entry by the medical officer states:

"Total incapacity for 6 months (If he lives as long)"

He was officially discharged from the army under Kings Regulation, Para.292 (xvi) "*No longer Fit for Service*" on the 19th August 1916 on a pension of 25/- per week.

Information received from the Plymouth Health Service Archive, Didworthy Sanatorium admission register states that:

"*Arthur William Parsons of Sennen, Penzance, Cornwall, noted as invalided soldier, age 26, single. It was noted that the disease first developed November 1914. He was admitted on 14 August 1916, and was sent there by Cornwall Insurance Commission.*"

He died at Didworthy Sanatorium on the 26th September 1916 and was buried in South Brent Cemetery. There is a notation of the Army Renewal or Revision of Pension Form that an invitation be sent to the War Grave Commissioner for a headstone.

Pvt Parsons headstone
Photo: Author's collection

The commission did provide a headstone of the standard pattern. Engraved with the badge off the 'The Royal Defence Corps'.

The funeral was carried out by A. W. Cranch of South Brent, the invoice shows the type of coffin supplied, and services rendered the cost and finally the location of the grave. The bill was paid on the 28th September 1916. His death was registered in Totnes.

Arthur is also commemorated on the Sennen war memorial, (4th from the bottom) at Lands' End. There is no rank or regimental details on the Memorial.

Sennen war memorial
Photo by Bob Harris

The army records show that after the death of Arthur, the army cancelled his pension, the wording is:

"*Cancel award from end of week in which man died*".

Arthur's father wrote to the army requesting any medals awarded to his son be sent to him. His letter reads:

Sir

Being the father of Arthur William Parsons, who joined up for the War. I wonder if I should have any medals belonging to him. No. 7390 Private Arthur William Parsons, who served for 306 days who died 26th September 1916 at the sanatorium, Didworthy South Brent Devon.

Yours Obediently
E.Parsons.

This letter was dated 27th Jan 1922. It was passed to O/c Number 8 district, with the notation, "*Passed to you, please*" and date stamped 28th Jan 1922.

The reply from the London Infantry Records, is dated 3rd March 1922. It is as follows:

Sir,

With reference to your letter dated January 27th. I have to inform you that your late son was not entitled to the award of any Distinctions yet for issue for services during the late War, as he did not serve overseas.

I am, Sir,

Your Obedient Servant,

Coronal
I/c Infantry Records,
London

Arthur was awarded the Home medal only. Arthur, like so many, died not in action but as a result of disease. There is the possibility that he was not properly medically examined on entry to the army, and that he was suffering from the early signs of TB. The possible reason for him being passed fit for service was that Kitchener wanted men to fight, at any cost.

Chapter Five

Many men went from South Brent to join the Colour's and returned home. From my research, some (not all) of their names, numbers and ranks are in alphabetical order are as follows:

Andrews, Alfred George,
Pvt. 36123/107409 Labour Corps.

Andrews, Thomas Ernest,
Pvt. 204279 R.E. 52798. Northumberland Fusiliers.

Barter, Harry,
15102, Grenadier Guards, 436714 Labour Corps. ** wounded

Beer, Archibald, Augustus James.
555, Sgt. Royal Flying Corps. (Died 1942 Malta. Flt. Lt. RAF.)

Brenton, George Henry,
47968/ LR/13/22594. Pvt. Bedford Regt.

Brenton, Fredrick,
2011/ 60037. Royal Regt. Of Artillery, R.G.A. Corps.

Butcher, Edward. G.
Lt. Northhants Regt. (Wounded Twice)

Collins, F.C.
Capt. MC. R.F.A. 17th. Ammunition Col.

Crispin Arthur Lockhart,
Pte. A.S.C. (M.T) M2/048452

Crispin, Fredrick Alfred.
Pte. 2264 MM. RAMC.

Crispin, William. Charles,
P.O. 233527, Royal Navy.

Crispin Walter Stumbles,
Sapper, 2989/560505. R.E.

Dodd, William.
Pte. 1100, Royal Horse Guards

Dodd, David,
P.O. Royal Navy, HMS Colossus

Dodd, Francis.
P.O. Royal Navy, HMS Pelorus.

Doddridge, Sydney George,
2364/ 240676. Devon Regt. Pvt. (Wounded) **

Doddridge, Fredrick William,
301607, Durham Light Infantry, Pvt. (Wounded)

Goss, Alfred, Pte.
15490, The Devon's.

Goss, Edwin, Pte.
37591 Somerset Light Infantry.

Hall, Charles,
Pte. 29729/186941.Devon's/ Labour Corps.

Hall, Walter.
Gnr. 1035 Devon R. G. A. **

Hard, Alfred Scott.
Royal Marines.

Hard, Charles,
Pte. 3460, 4th Devon's.

Hard, Richard, Charles,
Pte. 12033, Devon's/RE.

Hard, Robert James.
Pte. 52730/99829. Devon's/Labour.

Hard, Walter,
Pte. ASC/MT/285152. Army Service Corp.

Joint, Charles.
Petty Officer Stoker, Royal Navy

Joint, Richard.
Cpl. 239156/WR265111. RE. Railways. M.M

Kingwell. Fabyan Sparke Amery,
M1/5797. Sgt. ASC. (Pay Corps) Meticulous Medal

Lang, Charles William,
Pvt. 26679 9th Devon's **

Lang, Jarvis Henry.
Sgt. WR/208078. 173 Railway Co.

Langford, Edward Gilliat,
D.S.O. Lt. Col. 115 R.F.A.

Piper, John.
Royal Marines.

Richards, A.T.
Capt. R.G.A.

Scott, Alfred John.
Not Known

Shillabeer, Alfred.
Pte. 26124

Shillabeer, Charles.
Pte.2390/245581. Labour Corps.

Shillabeer, Sam J.
Pte.20041/247423. Devon's/Labour Corps

Smallridge, Fredrick.
29729/87986.Devons/32 M.G.C.

Winter, William Arthur.
Royal Flying Corps.

Waycott, J.F.G.
Sgt. 109983. 57th Field Bakery, ASC

(Silver Badge Holders, see appendix 5.)**

Chapter Six

Men from South Brent who Enlisted with the Colonial Forces

The following list is those men from the village who had emigrated to either Australia or Canada and chose to join the colonial regiment's and fight in Europe or the Balkans. All these men survived the Great War and returned to their adopted countries.

Australian Imperial Force

Abbott, Fernley, G.
Cpl. 1112 10th Batt. 3rd. Brigade Australian Imperial Forces. (Wounded Dardanelles Gun shot and shrapnel)

Waycott, Frank Ferris
Pte. 6424 Australian Imperial Forces. (Wounded, Shell Shock, returned sick to Australia)

Waycott, George, Percy, M.M.
Pvt. 3252, 8/57th Bat. Australian Imperial Forces.

Canadian Expeditionary Force

Goss, Thomas Owen. Pvt. 80028, 31st Battalion, Canadian Expeditionary Force.

Goss, Samuel Albert, Sgt. 18505, 2nd Bat. Canadian Infantry, Eastern Ontario Regt. Canadian Expeditionary Force.

Rogers, Claude, MM 186226, Pvt. 90th Winnipeg Rifles, Canadian Expeditionary Force.

Tozer, William, Henry. Pvt. 835176. 146 Canadian Expeditionary Force. 95th Battalion.

Chapter Seven

Bravery Awards to Men from South Brent

The next five pages list the Military Awards and distinctions won by the men and women from South Brent.

The Military Cross

Captain F. C. Collins,
Royal Field Artillery, 17th Divisional Ammunition Column, Third Army.

Lt. Stanley Richard
9th Machine Gun Corps.

The Military Medal Awarded to:

Private F. Crispin.	Royal Army Medical Corps.
L/Cpl. B.C. Hard.	Machine Gun Corps.
Corporal R. Joint,	Royal Engineers, Railway Troop.
Private C. Rogers,	Canadian Regiment
Pte. G. P. Waycott.	Australian Imperial Forces
E. Yeo.	Unit details unknown.

The Oak Leaf for 'Mentioned in Dispatches'

The 'Oak Leaf' is sown diagonally on to the Victory medal Ribbon for those who were 'Mentioned In Dispatches' during the Great War.

Miss Laura Moysey,
QAIMNS. Salonica, from Avonwick

Sergeant Farrier Hearly Hawkins,
13th Canadian Field Artillery.

Sergeant Samuel Goss,
2nd Batt. Eastern Ontario Regt. C.E.F.

War Medals Issued to All Men Who Served

These are the medals issued by the War Office. Men received either all or some of them depending when they enlisted and where they served, and a tunic ribbon.

1914 Star, British War Medal, Victory Medal.
(Left to right)
Collectively known as
'Pip, Squeak and Wilfred'

The Silver Badge

This badge was awarded to all of those military personnel who had served at home or overseas during the war, and who had been discharged from the army under King's Regulations (KR). 392(xvi), meaning the soldier had been released on account of being permanently physically unfit. The Badges are individually numbered so the recipient could be traced.

Harry Barter,	Badge No. B273660
Sydney George Doddridge,	Badge No. B268366
Walter Hall,	Badge No. 115126
Charles William Lang,	Badge No. 315595
Leonard Howard Shillabeer,	Badge No. 253022

Chapter Eight

Conclusion

The ceremony of Remembrance is still held in the village of South Brent and every other town and village across the land, in November, to packed Church's. The nation is led by the Queen at Sir Edward Lutyens Cenotaph in Whitehall, London. Similar ceremonies are carried out at War Memorials, large and small, throughout the land led by the Clergy and local dignitaries.

There is one memorial from South Brent which has been missing for many years. It is a brass plate mounted on an English oak base. The work was carried out by Mr J.Cole. The memorial bears the names of five soldiers from South Brent who died in the conflict. They were members of the Odd Fellows Lodge, Alexandria 5236, who met in the Pack Horse pub. The memorial was unveiled in April 1920.

There are now no survivors left from the Great War, the last being Private Harry Patch, of the Duke of Cornwall's Light Infantry, immortalised in the book "*The Last Fighting Tommy*". Yet there are still some children, now in the twilight of their years of those Soldiers, Sailors and Air man who remember their father's with affection.

There are many who will remember the Second World War which involved themselves, their relation and friends. More recently, there are villagers who have relatives and friends who have been in more recent conflicts of the late 20th. And the early 21st century, the Falkland War, The Balkans Conflict, The 1st and 2nd Iraq Wars and the Afghanistan. War.

I set out to find out who were the men and women from South Brent who died during the Great War. On this journey I have discovered that they were from all walks of life, some from the professions, some trades men, others from the farms.

The Western Times of September 10th 1920 quoted a man from Chumleigh, who at the dedication of the village war memorial, told the crowd, of the men who had died in the war:

'*They left their quiet homes in the country side at the call of arms to fight an arrogant and cruel enemy. They fought like men, they suffered like men and they died like men. Most families in the town had lost dear ones in the war. They bore their sorrow in silence and to them our deepest sympathy was extended*'. [1]

Henry Allingham, an Air Mechanic with the Naval Air Service during the Great War, said that:

"*It was the men in the trenches who won the war. What they put up with, no one will ever know. I've seen them coming out of the line, poor devils, in a terrible state, plastered with mud. They were like hermit crabs with all their equipment on and they would plonk down in the middle of the road before someone would pick them up*".[2]

My research into the soldiers of the Great War from South Brent has found six men who originated from the village, fought in the war and died. Their names have not been recorded on the Church memorial plaque. It is hoped that a centenary plaque will be commissioned and their named entered upon it before the centenary of the end of the war in 2019.

NOTES

1 Western Times 10th September 1920

2 Henry Allingham, 12 Sqd. Royal Naval Air Service, WW1

Chapter Nine

Postscript

The Parochial Church Council held its regular monthly meeting in March 2015. On the agenda for discussion was the possibility of erecting a centenary memorial and have the names of the men from South Brent who are not mentioned on the original memorial. The suggested design for the memorial was produced, in photographic form, and approved in principle. The working sculpture will be produced by Wendy Bristow.

At a P.C.C. meeting in July 2015, the finished bronze plaque was shown to the council members, and met with their full approval. The design was taken from a print of a painting by James Clarks called '*The Great Reward*' sent to the families of all those who died in the conflict. It first appeared in a magazine called 'The Graphic'.[1] The following quotation was also printed:

'*The sufferings of the present time are not worthy to be compared with the glory which will be revelled in us*' (Romans 8: 18.)

The Great Reward by James Clark

The Great Reward, painted by James Cark (1857-1943), was commissioned in April 1917 by The Graphic Magazine, a weekly illustrated magazine in direct completion to the illustrated London News. Clark also designed a number of war memorials and his painting was the basis for several memorial stained glass windows in churches. For more information on James Clark's paintings and life, go to **www.lizandarcy.co.uk**.

Proposed bronze design for centenary memorial

In August 2015, the South Brent Parish Church applied to the diocese for a facility to erect the centenary monument. A lower name plaque has to be added for the additional names of men who died during the Great War of 1914 – 1918.

NOTES

[1] The Graphic was a British Weekly Illustrated newspaper that was first published in December 1869.

Bibliography

Atkinson, C.T. *The Devonshire Regiment, 1914-1918.* Vol. 1 & 2. Eland Brothers, London. 1926.

Bidwell, Shelford & Dominic Graham. *Fire Power, British Army Weapons and Theories of War 1904-1945, London,* George Allen & Unwin (1982)

Brown, I.M. *British Logistics on the Western Front, 1914-1919,* Praeger Publishing, Wesport, USA, (1998)

Burt, R.A. *British Battleships 1889-1904.* Annapolis Maryland Naval Institute Press.1988

Campbell, David. *The 2nd Canadian Divisions: 'A Most Spectacular Battle'* Winifred Laurier University Press. 2007

Chichester, H. & Burges-Short, G. *The Records and Badges of Every Regiment and Corps in the British Army.* Second Ed. Gales and Polden Ltd. Aldershot. 1900

Churchill, R. Winston Churchill, *Young Statesman 1901-1914,* Heinemann Ltd. London, (1967)

Cook, Tim. *The Gunners of Vimy Ridge*, 2007.

Corbett, Julian S. *Naval Operations Vol. 1-5,* Longmans Green & Co. Second Ed. 1938.

Gray, T. *Lest Devon Forgets.* The Mint Press, Exeter, 2010.

Grieves, K. *Sir Eric Geddes, Business and Government in War and Peace,* Manchester University Press, Manchester (1989)

McGill, Harold. W. *Medicine and Duty, The World War 1 Memoir of Captain Mc Gill, Medical Officer 31st Battalion C.E.F.* 2007.

Nicholson, G.W.L. The Gunners of Canada, Vol.1 1534-1919.

Pallant, Ann. *A Sporting Century, 1863-1963.* Penwell Ltd, Callington, Cornwall, 1997

Parker, D. *The People of Devon in the First World War.* The History Press, Gloucester, 2013.

Pratt, E. *British Railways and the Great War: Organisation, Efforts, Difficulties and Achievements, vol. 1*, Selwyn and Blount Ltd, London. (1921)

Pratt, E. *British Railways and the Great War: Organisation, Efforts, Difficulties and Achievements, vol. 2*, Selwyn and Blount Ltd, London. (1921)

Regan, Geoffrey. *The Guinness Book of Military Blunders*, Guinness Publishing Company, London. Reprinted 1995.

Sheldon, Jack. *The German Army on Vimy Ridge 1914-1917*. Pen and Sword, Barnsley. 2008.

Taylor, A.J.P. *English History 1914-1945,* Oxford University Press, (1965)

Taylor, A.J.P. *The First World War. An Illustrated History*, Penguin Boos London, 1966.

Turner Alwyn, W. The Last Post, Music, Remberance and the Great War, Aurum Press, 2014. (Extract from Daily Mail, 7th November 2014)

Van Emden, Richard, *The Last Fighting Tommy, The Life of Harry Patch, Last Veteran of the Trenches, 1898-2009*. Bloomsbury Publishing, London, 2007.

Young, M. *Army Service Corps. 1902-18,* Second Edition, Partizan Press, Nottingham, (2012)

Wall, Greg, *The Book of South Brent,* Halgrove, Publishing, Tiverton, Devon, 2005

Wilson, Trevor. *The Myriad Faces of War; Britain and the Great War, 1914-1918*, Cambridge: Policy Press (1985)

Archival Material

The Fortescue Papers, Devon Heritage Centre, Exeter.
Plymouth City Archives
The Totnes and Mid Devon News,
(*Now known as the Totnes Times.*)
South Brent Parish Council Minutes.
Flight Magazine June 1918. Causality List.
The Aero plane Magazine 1918
Flight and Aircraft Engineer Magazine, January 1918
Supplement to the London Gazette May 1918
Harrow Memorial to the Fallen, Vol. VI
Mrs R. Cranch business archives.
Mrs B. Eales family Archive.
Mrs J. Sandry Family Archive
Ms Diana Goodman, The Rowland Archive

National Archives References

WO372 Medal Cards.
Australian National Archives, Cambria.
Canadian Archive, Canada Bok, 1829, Page 71 No. 489

Photographs

Mr Mike Sampson
Archivist, Blundell's School, Tiverton Devon
Mr Conrad Heath, South Brent Devon
Mr Michael Paget, Throwleigh, Devon
Mr William Douglas, Douglas Archives
Ms Diana Goodman, Rowlands Archives (USA)
Angelia Young, Rowlands Archives, USA
Mr Bob Harrison, Paul Church Archivist, Cornwall
Mr Tony Milton, Gribble Archives
Mrs Lynette Gribble, Gribble Archivist
The Author

Index